BEYOND DIVINE INTERVENTION

The Biology of Right and Wrong

John H. Morgan

BEYOND DIVINE INTERVENTION
The Biology of Right and Wrong

John H. Morgan
Ph.D.(Hartford), D.Sc.(London), Psy.D.

Library of Congress
LOC 2009940469

ISBN 1-55605-398-3
978-155605-3986

Wyndham Hall Press
5050 Kerr Rd.

Lima, Oh 45806

John H. Morgan

Published on the occasion of the 150th anniversary of
Charles Darwin's *Origin of Species* (1859).

"...as far as I know, no one has approached it
(moral development)
Exclusively from the side of natural history.

---Charles Darwin
Descent of Man (1871)

"The immediate need is for the scientific study of values."

---Julian Huxley
Evolutionary Humanism (1964)

"...(since) morality evolved as instinct ... science may soon
be in a position to investigate the very origin and meaning of
human values, from which all ethical pronouncements ...
flow."

---Edward O. Wilson
On Human Nature (1978)

Beyond Divine Intervention

To Edward O. Wilson,
whose life's work has captured
my imagination and provoked
this outburst of enthusiasm.

John H. Morgan

ACKNOWLEDGMENTS

Particular gratitude is expressed to

Harvard University

where I first encountered the work of Edward O. Wilson
during a postdoctoral appointment as a Visiting Scholar and
to

Oxford University

where I have had the privilege of teaching
a doctoral-level seminar on
Wilson's primary works.
Finally, to

Cambridge University

where I have recently been invited
to teach a course at
Madingley Hall.

Beyond Divine Intervention

TABLE OF CONTENTS

INTRODUCTION

In the following, we will consider three schools of thought, namely, ethical theism (which includes Jewish, Christian, and Islamic ethics), ethical humanism, and ethical naturalism. The first school of thought is based upon the Abrahamic faiths of Judaism, Christianity, and Islam. Though all are theocentric, the Christian perspective, it seems, must be distinguished from the high theocentrism of the rabbinic tradition of modern Judaism. Islamic ethics, on the other hand, is so far removed from Judaeo-Christian thought that it seems imperative that we treat this third theocentric ethical system quite separate and distinct. The second school of thought, namely, ethical humanism, is captured in the epic work of Sir Julian Huxley's great classic, *Evolutionary Humanism*. Finally, the third school of ethical thought, what we have chosen to call ethical naturalism, is fundamentally expressed in the monumental work of Edward O. Wilson, *On Human Nature*.

The intent in this study is to demonstrate a progression of human thought, beginning with the ethically mandated notion of ethical theism that "the Divine says," to a more sophisticated notion of humanism that "Man says," ending with the even more developed notion of naturalism that "the Earth says." We are, of course, set upon demonstrating a natural progression, a movement in maturity of thought if you will, from a God-centered "theocentricism" to a Man-centered "anthropo- centricism" to an Earth-centered "cosmocentricism."

Lest the reader make the unfortunate and incorrect assumption that these three terms are universally recognized categories of ethical inquiry, let me say here immediately that these are three terms which I myself have chosen as handles for these three schools of thought. To my certain knowledge, they have not been universally employed in this manner before. However, that being said, I will argue that the three categories are most helpful and easily used in discussions of ethical schools of thought. For the reader desiring a wider berth of resources in the refinement of ethical schools of thought beyond the three identified here, I have included a resource bibliography based upon the work of G. J. Warnock, a Fellow of Magdalen College, Oxford University. For our purposes here, nevertheless, we will adhere to the three schools of thought which I have chosen to label ethical theism (theocentric ethics), ethical humanism (anthropocentric ethics), and ethical naturalism (cosmocentric ethics).

In many respects, this inquiry is a further extension of my earlier work, *Naturally Good: A Behavioral History of Moral Development* (2005), which assumed a natural history of ethical evolution within the human community. In this present study, I go further and argue that the moral code is not just intrinsic to the human animal but is derived from nature itself.

Theocentric ethics, as a school of thought called here "ethical theism," is based on the belief that the moral code for human behavior has been derived externally from the human condition, that is, it has been "divinely revealed" through the intervention of a God who stands outside but is yet interested in the world and its affairs. This is as true of Judaism and Islam as it is of Christianity, though in each tradition, there is an extremely wide berth of variations as to exactly how this "divine intervention" has occurred and what its present relationship is to the universe generally and humankind specifically.

Anthropocentric ethics, as a school of thought called here "ethical humanism," is based on the belief that the moral code for human behavior is derived from within the human experience itself. Following Darwin, there is the conviction that moral behavior is a biologically derived code of conduct generated from the inevitabilities of genetic and speciel survival. *(Note: Throughout this book, I use the word "speciel" as an adjective form of the noun "species." I am aware that I have created the term myself but I am unrepentant in that I believe it conveys a concept which presently is not named elsewhere.)* In other words, whereas theocentric ethics is externally derived from a divine source, anthropocentric ethics is an internal derivative of the human experience itself. Humankind has developed its own code of moral conduct based upon the experiential matrix of biological survival and, therefore, we must look to ourselves for moral guidance rather than looking to a non-human source outside the universe .

Cosmocentric ethics, as a school of thought called here "ethical naturalism," is based on the conviction that the moral code for human behavior is derived from within the matrix of the cosmos rather than either from God (God says do this or that) or from humankind (Man says do this or that). Rather, a cosmocentric ethic is based upon the biologically validated reality that what is good for the world is good for all that is in it, including but not primarily humankind. I use the term "cosmos" rather than "earth" to suggest the universality of this ethical perspective for, though the earth is central to human experience, the earth is not the center of the universe and this ethical system seeks to be inclusive of all phenomenal existence. Practically speaking, however, we will use the term "cosmocentric" with special reference to the earth and the ecosystem of the earth upon which the concept of cosmocentric ethics is postulated. Not everyone will be happy with our mission and certainly not with our findings.

With respect to nomenclature, I have chosen to use the term "humankind" as often as literarily appropriate as a more broadly constructed term than "man" or even "mankind." Owing, of course, to the time period in which selected texts were written, it was predetermined that they would use the generic "man" as the comprehensive term for the human species. On rare occasions, however, I will myself use the term "Man" as an exact synonym for "humankind," as in the literarily more easily used phrase, "Man says" which then parallels the terms "God says" and "Earth says." This, I find, more linguistically balanced than the more cumbersome phrase, "Humankind says." I beg the pardon of the reader who feels offended by my position on this sensitive matter and invite them to make the mental transposition if it helps them avoid an unfortunate false assumption that this author is a chauvinist! Though denials often come from the blatantly guilty, I protest any suggestion that I have failed to demonstrate gender-sensitivity by employing this convenient, albeit simplistic, linguistic parsimony. I, nevertheless, stand by it.

Of course, before we can even hope to proceed with a reasonable discussion of ethics conceived theistically, humanistically, or naturalistically, we must first establish the definitional perimeters of our terms. To glibly speak of morals and ethics without saying exactly what we are suggesting by these terms is how many people, groups, governments, and religions get themselves into trouble. Let us, at least, be clear in our usage and in our prejudices. I understand "ethics" to be a reflection upon or, if you will, ideas about "morality," which, in turn, is behavior. Reflection upon action constitutes the matrix of morals and ethics. Morality is behavior answering the human quandary, "What to do" whereas ethics is reflection upon the question of "Why do it." The difference between saying a person is "moral" and saying a person is "ethical" is the difference between saying a person has "done" the right thing and a person has "thought" he has done the right thing.

The relationship between morals and ethics is very close, but distinct, even though many people discussing right and wrong behavior will, unfortunately and to the detriment of linguistic acuity, use them interchangeably. When a person is called moral and ethical in the same breath, chaos and confusion reign. What we are suggesting here is that "morality has to do with behavior" whereas "ethics has to do with thinking" about and reflecting upon an idea of what is right and wrong. A moral person responds to the challenge of "what to do" whereas an ethical person responds to the challenge of "what to do" with a reflective understanding of "why do it."

We might argue that a moral person is not necessarily "ethical" nor is an "ethical" person necessarily "moral." It is quite possible for a person to "do the right thing" without ever reflecting upon "why it was done," whereas it is equally possible for an individual to think about or reflect upon "why a thing should be done" without actually doing it. Piaget has written extensively upon this subject as relates to the moral development of children. I have, myself, written extensively upon this subject in my work on the behavioral history of moral development. It can be argued, though some will dispute it, that an individual who does the right thing without reflecting upon why it is, actually, the right thing to do is not, in reality, necessarily a moral person at all because the act of "doing the right thing" is integrally tied to an understanding of or reflection upon "why it is the right thing to do." In other words, is "doing the right thing" without thinking about the "doing of it" really moral behavior?

The relationship between behavior and ideology, therefore, is central to our discussion. Let us consider "behavior" itself. Behavior as judged in human terms is "action," whether that action be intentional, accidental, or reflexive. We will avoid the use of the term "instinctual" because today it is fraught with psychological and political baggage which I am neither willing nor interested in unpacking. But to say a human act falls within one of these three categories of actuation, namely, intentional, accidental, or reflexive, is quite defensible. (Note: I have discussed "reflexive cognition" in my 2007 book, *"In the Beginning...": Paleolithic Origins of Religious Consciousness*.) An act, we are saying, is either "on purpose," "inadvertent," or "a biogenic response" to a stimulus introduced either externally or internally to the human person.

We are here, then, faced in our discussion of "morality as behavior" with the prospects of an act done either (1) on purpose, (2) unintentionally and inadvertently, or (3) a mere biological response to a stimulus. In this case, it is conceivable that a moral act may occur without "reflection" by which we mean "intention." To do the right thing, the moral act, without intending to do it, as in the case of (2) and (3) above hardly makes for a moral act at all. The right thing was done but not on purpose, not intentionally, but merely by accident or reflex. So, we have the possibility of an individual doing the "moral" thing without thereby being characterized as a "moral" person. In the instances of (2) and (3), that is, accidentally or reflexively, the right things were done but the doing of them was not moral because "intention" was not present in the acts.

There are, of course, "gradations" of moral behavior or actions related to right and wrong, namely, moral, immoral, and amoral. Moral acts are those in which the "intent" is to do the right thing. Immoral acts are those in which the "intent" is NOT to do the right thing. Amoral acts are those in which there is no intent to do either the right or the wrong thing. In the case of "moral" acts, they are done on

John H. Morgan

purpose intending the right. In the case of "immoral" acts, they are done on purpose intending the wrong. In the case of amoral acts, they are done with no intention of either right or wrong.

Ethics, on the other hand, has nothing directly to do with "acts" or "behavior," but rather with "intentionality," for intentionality necessitates an address to the "why" of an act without it being the act itself. The idea of doing the right thing is quite different from doing the right thing. The former is of the nature of "ethics" whereas the latter is of the nature of "morals." One can be an outstandingly ethical person without being a moral person for one can reflect upon, ponder, and cogitate upon moral action without engaging in that action. However, one cannot be an outstandingly moral person without being an ethical person for moral action necessarily requires reflection upon, pondering, or cogitating upon moral action. One can have ethics without morality but not morality without ethics. If we don't keep this distinction clearly before us, what is to follow will be both difficult to grasp and impossible to accept. *Ethics, then, is ideology; morality is behavior.*

Now, before we proceed to an investigation of our three ethical systems, we might be well advised to note here that the entire basis upon which an ethical system and its moral expression exists has to do with the "source" of what is determined by that system to be considered right and wrong. An ethical system bases its entire validity upon this fundamental notion of the "source" of its discrimination as relates to its ideas about and behavior regarding right and wrong. These, we call, "domain assumptions." In short, we will argue that the domain assumption of ethical theism is that the source of determining what is right and wrong is derived from divine intervention, from God if you will, and

13

that moral behavior and ethical reflection have to do with what "God says" in revelation. The domain assumption of ethical humanism is that the source of determining what is right and wrong is derived from human reason and that doing the right thing is based strictly upon what "Man says" about what is right and wrong for people to do in the world. Finally, the domain assumption of ethical naturalism is that the source of determining what is right and wrong is derived from human scientific knowledge of the ecosystem of the universe and that doing the right thing is based strictly upon what the "Earth says" about what is right and wrong for the survival and endurance of the Cosmos, whether or not that ethical system and its moral consequences favor the survival of the human species.

Our intention, then, is to argue for a maturing process in ethical ideology and moral behavior, which began in human history with a reliance upon an intervening source of knowledge regarding what is right and wrong, called God, and moved to a more reflective notion of a source of knowledge regarding what is right and wrong based upon human reason, called Man, and, finally, to arrive at an ethical system of thought based upon scientific understanding of the environmental integrity of the cosmos as relates to what is right and wrong for the universe. From God, to Man, to Earth is the upwardly accelerating understanding of the need for and the nature of an ethical system based upon what is best for the Cosmos, what we have chosen to call ethical naturalism. Let us commence our inquiry and determine, at the end of the day, if we have succeeded in justifying our point.

John H. Morgan

CHAPTER ONE

ETHICAL THEISM
in the Thought of Judaism, Christianity, and Islam

Ethical Theism defines ethics as coming from outside the human experience. The human condition requires a "revealed" code of behavior. Ethics is what is prescribed by this revealed code of behavior. Morality is doing the right thing as determined by the revealed code. Moral behavior is doing the right thing because God said do it.

JEWISH THEOCENTRIC ETHICS

Geoffrey Wigoder's 1989 essay on theocentric ethics in the *Encyclopedia of Judaism* has been chosen for its fundamental freshness. Jewish in essentials, it speaks correctly of the essence of a "theocentric" ethics. Wigoder delves into the biblical concepts of ethics and morality while stirring clear of theological ethics in the Jewish tradition. Let me say here that Wigoder has made little distinction in the following discussion between the use of the terms "ethics" and "morals" and this failure, again, serves our purpose in explicating the fundamentals of an ethical system based upon God at the center.

Wigorder is quick to point out the "progressive" nature of the biblical narratives which cover centuries while always honoring the fundamentals of theistic ethics. He is particularly keen to identify the biblical sources of "divine" mandates as relates to scripted behavior in given situations which led, of course, to rabbinic extrapolations of moral principles. He is especially eager to emphasize the "good and just" characteristics of the God of the Bible, particularly when such Divine behavior seems to be anything but good or just. Ethical theism is astute at both contrasting human behavior with that of Divine behavior and then emphasizing the instructional nature of the latter for the former. Moral behavior comes from the human person emulating the actions of God Himself.

Even though the first five books of the Bible, known as the Pentateuch, constitute the repository of Jewish Law, which in their own fashion embody the moral components of Israel Divine mandate, the prophetic writings of Jewish scripture constitute the formal application to real-life situations, the *zeit geist* of the time of writing. Moral behavior constitutes the watermark of Israel's code of conduct embodied in the figures of historic narratives. The complimentarity of the social morality of the prophets is realized in the personal morality of the great biblical narratives. It is the wisdom literature which elevates and integrates social and personal morality into fundamental personality traits of the faithful.

The development of the moral code of the faithful is indicated in the stories which exemplify a reflective community's reliance upon an ethical self-understanding. The gradual emergence of "ethical principles" and "moral codes of behavior" are early exemplified in the historic narratives, wisdom literature, and the writing of the early prophets of Israel. Wigoder is suggesting that the Ten Commandments embody a certain deference to the moral codes and attribute to them special value within the community of the faithful.

Here, ethical theism is most conspicuously evidenced in biblical teaching. That the God of Creation is a moral

God, a God of eternal value, a God of justice and kindness but also one who embodies the qualities of mercy and forgiveness as essential components of His moral being is pervasive in the Pentateuch and the Prophets. It is through moral conduct that the human person encounters and cultivate a relationship with God. The fusing of the moral commands with individual and social behavior constitutes the work of rabbinic scholarship. The creative application of the moral commands to existential situations is indicative of rabbinic genius and the literature which grew from such creativity in fusing biblical commands and personal behavior is indicative of the Jewish capacity to honor the ancient texts while living in the real world.

Extrapolation was the mechanism whereby the rabbinic councils were able to move the biblical mandates into the daily lives of the Jewish people through the centuries. The quest for the "master principle in Jewish morality" has always been at the center of rabbinic reflection upon the centrality of the God of Creation to the everyday lives of the faithful. It was the *zeit geist* which constituted, for the rabbis, the matrix within which ethics and moral behavior were to be considered. How to fuse the ancient code with the modern experience of life, whether by modern we mean the early centuries of Judaism or of current times. Fusing the Divine mandates codified in the commandments with the real life situation of the faithful in every generation constitutes the rabbinic agenda. Needless to say, the "special qualities" of rabbinic teachings and Jewish morality have to do with the centrality of the God of Creation, the origin of all moral behavior and ethical codes.

The uniqueness of Judaism, it may be argued, is not just the involvement of God in the moral struggle but of Israel's claim to an individualized and personalized relationship to God. The biblical affirmation of God's personal involvement in the moral struggle of human existence is the central characteristic of ethical theism. The God of the Bible is the true source of morality and it is Israel, His chosen people, who is both the embodiment and the purveyor of that ethical code of conduct. Righteousness is derived from a belief in and adherence to the mandates of God as understood and interpreted by Israel through the rabbinic tradition of scholarship. Catholics would want to suggest that the explication of the Will of God and His moral mandates are derives from the Church's teachings as explicated by the Pope and his Bishops. Yet and still, whether Jewish or Catholic, the notion that the God of the Bible is the source and perpetrator of ethical codes and moral conduct is without question.

The ethical theism embodied in the monotheistic religions of Judaism, Christianity, and Islam, different as they are, embodies a behavioral matrix consisting of both "action" and "ideology," or, more simply, what one does is also important for why one does it. The doing of a good deed must be accompanied by a good intention. And, furthermore, morality is not just doing the right thing for the right reason but saying what it is one does and why is also central to ethical theism -- action, intentionality, and articulation. These constitute the matrix of biblical ethics.

Today, for example, the biblical sensitivity to animal life expressed in the rabbinic tradition and Talmudic mandates regarding their care, treatment, and function, has taken on a new relevance in the animal ethics movement, particularly for the progressive elements within Judaism. The giant step from animal sacrifices to animals ethics is explained in terms of a deepening understanding of the intentionality of the Law and not just its words. One need not be a vegetarian to care about the care and treatment of animals, say the ethical theists. The Bible as read and

John H. Morgan

understood by ethical theists, furthermore, embraces human dignity and the fundamental equality of all human beings. The ethnocentric racism which seems to be blatantly present throughout the early biblical stories are discounted in defending the God of Creation as a Just and Merciful God. Non-theists are called upon to wrestle with what otherwise appears to be bold contradictions between what is said about the loving God of monotheists (Jews, Christians, and Muslims) and what is said about the biblical God in Scripture.

Wigoder has explained a bit more what is meant by the rabbinic concept of the Noachide Laws. I quote here his brief explanation: "(The Noachide Laws consists of) even key rules of morality which, in the rabbinic view, are the duty of all mankind to obey as the descendants of a common ancestor. Traditionally imposed on Noah, these Noachide (or "Noachian") Laws preceded the Torah and the Halakhah -- the legal system meant only for the Jewish people. According to Maimonides, acceptance -- on the basis of the Bible -- of the seven universal precepts means that any such righteous Gentile is numbered with "the pious ones among the nations of the world (Haside ummot ha-olam) deserving a share in the world to come" (Tosef. Sanh. 13.2). (Here he lists the seven laws.) (1) civil justice (the duty to establish a legal system); (2) the prohibition of blasphemy (which includes the bearing of false witness); (3) the abandonment of idolatry; (4) the prohibition of incest (including adultery and other sexual offenses); (5) the prohibition of murder; (6) also that of theft; (7) the law against eating flesh ("a limb") cut from a living animal (I.e., cruelty in any shape or form). (TB Sanh. 56a)."

In an attempt to maintain absolute consistency in the portrayal of God as morality itself, ethical theists have taken the interesting position of suggesting that there is something that God cannot do, namely, God cannot do other than good. God is incapable of doing evil and human beings participate in this goodness by virtue of our free will and the fundamental composition of the human person, created to do good by a God who embodies goodness itself. The universality of biblical morality is without dispute among ethical theists. All human beings are bound by the same morality and, though the Jews are a chosen people, no human being is exempt from doing good for goodness is of our very nature. Here, of course, Jewish theology and Christian theology part company for Christians believe, contrary to Judaism and Islam, that the human person is born with Original Sin and, thus, even if there is the inclination to do good, the human person stands in need of an outside intervention in order to turn his will towards God to do the right thing. As Reinhold Neibuhr has said in an attempt to explain the Christian understanding of the relationship between "free will" and "original sin:" He has said, "Man does not sin necessarily, but inevitably"!

Certainly the Bible is replete with specific commandments, specific laws, specific and often detailed instructions about doing the right thing and not doing the wrong thing. Yet, in the rabbinic tradition (as well as Christian and Islamic traditions), there is an ancient practice of extrapolation from detail directives to general principles. To understand the Law of God is to understand these principles which serve to govern all of life's activities. The rabbinic tradition is one of continual development and expansion of these principles and their application. Here, more than any where else in our discussion, we see a parting of ways between the Jews and Christians on the one side the Muslims on the other for no Muslim would ever presume to suggest that it is the destiny of man to "become like God." This, as we shall see later, is the ultimate blasphemy of a theist! Yet, Jews and Christians, alike, embody this idea that being in the "image of God" is to seek to "become like Him."

CHRISTIAN CHRISTOCENTRIC ETHICS

In the previous discussion of ethical theism, we have focused upon the biblical tradition as articulated by rabbinic scholarship and, thus, is somewhat skewed to Judaism. Because Judaism is the oldest of the three western monotheistic traditions, it seems not unreasonable that we began there our discussion of the place of God in ethics and morals. Christian morality has a distinguishing characteristic which is not found, or only implicitly, outside the Christian faith, namely, the believer experiences moral obligations wholly and entirely in the light of God's grace and love. It is an obligation under God who is wholly and entirely love and who wills to save and direct the world by his grace and love in his only-begotten Son. Whether Jews and Muslims will permit this exclusive claim for Christian morality is a point for further and future discussion, but for now let it be registered that this is the essential position of the Christian tradition, namely, the ethical code and moral system embodied in Christianity is based solely upon God's grace and love for humankind. This total goodness, embodied in God himself, is made available to all human beings through the grace and love radiating from God through his Son, Jesus Christ. To miss the centrality of the Sonship of Jesus is to miss the whole point of Christianity for God is only and solely known to the human person through God's Son. This, needless to say, is radically divergent, even heretically offensive, to both Jews and Muslims.

Unlike the rabbinic tradition of insistence upon the "imitation of God" as the basis for Jewish ethics, Christians argue that it is only in knowing the person of Jesus Christ as God's Son that God's will can even be known by the human community.   Christianity is, then, based solely upon a "morality of imitation of Christ," and the reading of biblical ethics must always be within this context.   Christ is either present or anticipated in every biblical mandate for good and though this hermeneutic does violence to the Jewish understanding of the Torah and Prophets, it is the Christian community's insistence that nothing can be gleaned from the Scriptures except through the prism of Christian exegesis, an interpretative mechanism based upon the Sonship of Jesus of Nazareth.

Sharing with the rabbinic scholars an insistence that morality is based upon action, intentionality, and affirmation, Christianity insists that true morality generates love imitating the love of God for humanity by requiring the death of His own Son as a sacrifice through his life and death bringing "grace," not "law" to humanity.   Only within the Christian worldview does this make sense.

Unlike the rabbinic tradition of Judaism and the hadiths of Islam, Christianity suggests that natural law is in process, it is emerging in human consciousness as deepening understanding of the human person and the human community's growing relationship to God as revealed in the person of Jesus as Divine Son and Heir.   Whereas the Torah and the Qur'an are set, Christianity is in organic emergence based upon the continually increasing understanding of the Will of God as realized in the person of Jesus as interpreted by the Church fathers.   Christianity's work is never finished, it is always in motion, until the coming of Christ in the final judgment.

Interiority of accountability and exteriority of responsibility comprise the bookends of Christian moral behavior.   The emphasis, realized in the life and ministry of Jesus and epitomized in his willingness to die for others, is a duality of embrace.   One must be accountable ontologically

John H. Morgan

and one must likewise be responsible existentially. Whether or not this is unique to Christianity over against Judaism and Islam is very much open to debate but the impetus for this duality of accountability and responsibility, for the Christian, is centered in Christ as Lord and Savior. That is clearly the basis for Christian ethics.

When ethical theism expresses itself in Christian thought, the monumental difference between Christianity and the Jewish and Islamic traditions become crystal clear. Though all three traditions fall within the monotheistic belief in one God, the similarities stop there. For Catholics, the strong belief that faith is a gift from God bringing with it a new life in Christ, not just a new morality, is fundamental. This new life introduces the believer to a relationship with the Triune God, namely, Father, Son, and Holy Spirit. This new life is a Divine gift available to all who will accept it.

Though salvation is by grace through faith, the believer is under obligation to discharge a life of service and obedience. That salvation is a gift does not diminish the necessity of doing one's duty to God and humankind. For Catholics, doing the right thing is not enough. One must accept God's gift of grace through accepting God's Son, living the Christian life in Christ Jesus. Salvation comes, not by good works, by good works follow the believer in Christ. Without this belief, good works mean nothing. Here Catholics part company with both the Jewish and Islamic traditions in which good deeds are themselves meritorious by virtue of being done and not based strictly upon a faith commitment.

In spite of the Church's teaching that salvation is through grace by faith, there are a plethora of things one must do and things one must not do in order to receive salvation. This litany of behavioral constraints and mandates do not diminish, the Church teaches, the fact that salvation is a gift from God, a gift one must receive willingly.

The burden of obedience is lightened, the Church teaches, by the will of Christ to those who accept him as Lord and Savior. The Gospels are not merely guidelines, they constitute the framework for a set of fundamental principles which the Church and her bishops have interpreted for the believer. Obeying the will of God is accepting the teachings of the Church and obeying the precepts of Christ interpreted by the Church.

Catholics believe and the Church teaches that if one truly loves God by following Jesus Christ, that individual will do the right thing. Doing the right thing is the sign that one loves God and is a follower of Christ. "If you love me," Jesus said, "you will obey my commandments." The Church teaches that salvation is a free gift of God's grace to any who will accept His Son as Lord and Savior, yet, in order to be saved, one must follow the rules laid down by the Church as interpreted from the Gospels.

The obedience of the Ten Commandments must be matched by a belief in Christ as God's Son, otherwise, that obedience to the Law is meaningless for the gift of grace must be received by the believer and that gift is predicated upon the divinity of Christ. One must love God and Man as a sign of salvation, but salvation is only available to those who love God and Man through the medium of Jesus Christ. All else is meaningless.

Christians teach and believe that love is the fundamental principle of obedience to the Will of God. Yet, this love is only real in those who have accepted the belief in the Triune God and the divinity of God's Son, Jesus Christ. Any other belief is futile and all expressions of love of God and Man come to naught in the absence of a believe in Christ as Lord.

Since it is not what one does that assures salvation

but what one believes, those who accept Christ as Lord and Savior are led to do the right thing because of the acceptance of God's gift of grace through Jesus. For those who fail to accept Jesus, they thereby reject the gift of God's grace and, thus, their acts of love are of no value, are really expressions of the defiance of God for refusing to accept his Son Jesus Christ. Action and intentionality are governed by the rightness of one's love, a love which comes from a personal knowledge of God through Jesus Christ. This is the love that motivates the true believer to do the right thing.

The complexity of moral decision making is, in the Catholic tradition, such that one must rely upon the teachings of the Church and the interpretation of the Scriptures by the traditions of the Church in order to make sure one is doing the right thing. Dependence upon one's own personal understanding, as in Protestantism, will never do for Catholics. It is the Church who is invested with the authority of Scriptural interpretation and the priests, bishops, and pope must constitute the final court of authority in all matters of moral judgment.

The Christian church is adamant in its understanding of moral directives and is unrelenting in its assertion that the Church is the arbiter of judgment when it comes to moral behavior and ethical precepts. The individual cannot, must not, may not be empowered to exercise his or her own judgment in moral decision making. The Church as the medium of God's Will must be listened to and obeyed.

Christians do not believe in the exercise of individual judgment in matters affecting a moral precept. One must, even when it appears to be unfair or unfeeling or uncaring, obey the teachings of the Church and her clergy for it is the Church which is empowered with the right of interpreting moral precepts and it is the Church that instructs and controls all those who would receive God's gift of grace through acceptance of Jesus Christ and obedience to Christ's Church.

The tradition of martyrdom within the Catholic Church is built upon the precept that there are some things that must never be done under any circumstances whatsoever. It is the Church and her bishops who determine what those things are as they interpret the Gospels and serve as arbiters of God Will in the world. The power of the Church's authority must not be questioned but, when obeyed, one can be certain that he or she is doing the Will of God through Christ because the Church is the "Bride of Christ," the embodiment of the Will of Christ. Christ is the "fullness of God," for he is the embodiment of both the Will of God and the Way of God for all mankind. To obey Christ as interpreted by the Catholic Church is to assure one's salvation.

The Christian's motive for doing the right thing is to please God by manifesting a love which has grown from an encounter with Christ as Lord. Christians must do the right thing to show they love God and by following the life of Christ one shows that love. Without Christ, there is no God and without God there is no love.

ISLAMIC THEOCENTRIC ETHICS

The following is a short running commentary on a splendid article by Dr. Jamal Badawi entitled, "The Foundation of Islamic Ethics" from a lecture series on Islamic Teaching. Though Badawi does not bother to make the distinction between "ethics" and "morals" as I have been doing in this discussion, "morals," he does points out, "can either be classified as secular or religious." Secular morality tries to establish a moral system that is independent of God and religious faiths. As for religious morality, it is fundamentally based on two things; first is the belief in God as the Creator of the universe, and second is the belief in the Hereafter. "Religious morality" is not a uniformly used term because the fundamentals of religious morality are not the same for all religions.

Islam is quite profoundly the "monotheistic" religion because it is outspokenly non-compromising when it comes to the unity and sovereignty of God. Though we know many attributes of God, there is no hint of human beings "becoming God" or even being a "co-creator with God" as suggested in the mysticism of Judaism and Christianity.

The Will of God is singular, uncorrupted with humanlike emotions, and is constituted of His divine attributes. Whereas in Judaism, we see a God who is jealous, gets angry, takes revenge, as we do in the Christian scriptures, Islam has no such notion. The Will of God is undifferentiated in its singularity, consistency, and applicability.

The notion of an intermediary between God and man is abhorrent to Muslims for it breaches the one-to-one relationship which God offers to every single individual in the world. Furthermore, there is genuine opportunity for the oneness of God to be decidedly compromised by the idea of an intermediary between God and every individual.

Islamic scholars are frustrated but patient with the naïve notion among both Jews and Christians that their idea of God is the same as the Muslim concept of God. For a Muslim, the notion that God is simply a further and later interpolation of the biblical God is not only wrong but offensive in its simplemindedness. The potential or latent polytheism implied in the Christian doctrine of the Trinity (three gods but one!) is matched by the naïve portrayal of the Jewish God as tribal or super-human in character. All such notions are alien to Islam. The purity and singularity of God

27

is never questions, never adulterated, never compromised. "These descriptions," explains Badawi, "that depict God as a super-human being contradict Islam's emphasis on God's transcendence, His total freedom from all human defects, and that He is not human-like because He is not 'physical' in the sense that He can be perceived." Seeing God, touching God, being familiar with God as portrayed in both the Jewish and Christian scriptures is both alien and offensive to Muslims. The sovereignty of God is never questioned, never altered, and always present in any discussion of the God of Islam.

"If the Islamic concept of God." suggests Badawi, "is compared with the Biblical concept of the 'God of Israel,"\' we find that the first chapter in the Qur'an describes God as 'Lord of the universe' (Al-Fatihah 1:2), and the last chapter of the Qur'an describes Him as 'Lord of mankind' (An-Nas 114:1). The Qur'an does not say 'God of Arabs' or 'God of Muslims' or God of any ethnic group, but God is the God of all humanity." Once again, the Jewish notion of God, and by extension the Christian notion, is that God is the God of Creation but in some special sense is first and foremost the God of the Israelites. The doctor of God as expounded by the teachings of Islam is that God is the God of the universe, he is not a tribal God, a God of a single people, or a God who could even conceivably imagine a preference of one peoples over another. An ethnic God is alien to Islam.

The Muslims take the day when arguing for their notion of the singularity and oneness of God. Whereas Jews and Christians have their special access to their God, Muslims affirm and pronounce the universality of God. It is radical, pure monotheism. To propose a Son of God other than all human beings as God's children is quite decidedly offensive, naïve, and heretical to Muslims.

"The concept of God in Islam," continues Badawi, "affects its ethical system in many ways." Divided loyalties between God, His Son, the Holy Spirit, the Saints, Mary the Mother of Heaven, etc., is inconceivable to a Muslim. God is one. There is no God but God. All others and all else are less than and will never be equal to God. The attribution of human frailties to the character and behavior of God is blasphemy! To propose that a human being is the Son of God is blasphemy! Jesus is a prophet and teacher of men. He is not God, nor any part of God more than any other human being participates in the love and will of God.

Here, then, is the essence of Islamic ethics. The moral code of conduct is dictated by a belief that God knows all, He sees all, and that every believer in God and obedient servant of God must obey the Will of God for God knows all. There is no hiding; there is escape.

Muslims are not afraid of success; they are not afraid of wealth and prosperity. Whereas in Christianity, there is always the notion that wealth and prosperity can become distractions from doing the Will of God, Islam emphasizes how these gifts of prosperity and wealth are instruments of service to God. Whereas the Christian tradition often looks askance at the successful, Muslims believe that this is a sign of God's blessing and that such blessings should and must be used to the glory of God and in His service. There is no tradition of celibacy, no tradition of monkish deprivation, but rather of outgoing service in the name of God.

Salvation is to be earned. It is not given as a gift for believing in God. Grace is not a central doctrine within Islam, but rather good works and servanthood in service to the Will of God. Salvation is to be worked for and not simply expected. The exercise of justice and peace in the world is the means to assure Salvation.

Another outstanding Islamic scholar today is Majid Fakery and his article, "Ethics in Islamic Philosophy" from his Ethical Theories in Islam constitutes the focus of our attention now because Fakery extends and elaborates the discussion of morality in Badawi's work and places much more emphasis upon the "systemics of ethical deliberation" as well as their "moral application." He is considered, like Badawi, a major spokesperson for the teachings of Islam and is particularly distinguished in his understanding of the history of Islamic ethics and the moral code. I have used his "Arabic" Anglicizations as well as English translations in my attempt to honor the integrity of his own text to which I offer modest commentary in italics.

Fakery is refreshingly non-defensive in his recognition and acknowledgement of the historic origins of Islamic thought which drew quite decidedly from the Greek philosophers (as did many Jewish and Christian thinkers as well). The realization that no ideas are truly and solely original when it comes to philosophical speculations about ethics and moral behavior, Fakery easily identifies and traces the line of development from one generation to the next and one thinker to the next, including in the mix the profound impact of Greek thought on Islamic formulations.

The gradual emergence of a philosophically sophisticated notion of right and wrong caused a disturbance within the Islamic community of scholars. One school was insistent upon the notion that right and wrong are solely and singularly defined by God and doing right and doing wrong was equated with doing the will of God. However, the philosophers of the Mu'tazilite school of Basra and Badhdad wished to develop an ontological notion of right and wrong, that which in the very essence of being could and does determine right and wrong. Their argument was that by so doing, they were able to demonstrate the philosophical sophistication of the teachings of Islam for the ontological will of God was ultimately the source of ethics.

Here, not unlike what happened in the Christian and

subsequently the Jewish traditions of theology, Islam came in contact with and conflict with Greek philosophy. Whereas the traditionalists, namely the Mu'tazilites, wish only to stay with the Qur'an and the hadiths of the Prophet, Al'Kindi, the first truly philosophical ethicist within Islam, wish to embrace Greek philosophy and its metaphysical categories for defining and defending ethics and moral behavior.

Islam will for centuries wrestle with the problematic of the introduction of Greek philosophy into the teachings of Islam. The high profile of Plato is not to be questioned for he is acclaimed by many a Muslim scholar as the apex of wisdom and insight into the nature of being. Plato's psychology, his definitions of the soul and the components which make up the human person, were embraced by many Muslim scholars, particularly and early by Abu Bakr al-Razi, and this movement towards Patonic categories has characterized much of Islamic theology ever since.

Al'Razi's emphasis upon "reason" as the paramount human characteristic suggests the influence of Plato on Islamic speculation. It is "reason," not passion or the hedonistic life of self-indulgence which determines the direction of a person's life towards God.

Here is a notion not fully embraced by the major schools of thought in Islam, namely, reincarnation. Yet, al'Razi and al'Kindi do not discount the possibility of individuals returning to this world after death. Death, however, they argue is a defining characteristic of the human person and this does become a central teaching of Islam. Death is as characteristic of the human person as life and love. But in death, the human person meets God and answers God for the life he has chosen to live, whether good or bad. Whereas al'Kindi was the first philosopher of ethics in Islam, al'Farabi was the first systematic philosophical thinker, one who particularly set out to create a philosophical system of thought conversant with the Greeks and compliant with Islam teaching. He is particularly dependent or at least obliged to the work of Aristotle as relates to the fundamental human virtues, practical and intellectual. The reliance upon the Greeks, especially Aristotle, has always been both evident and acknowledged by Islamic scholars. Al'Farabi, for example, is most dependent upon the nuancing of the concept of justice in the works of Aristotle and his insights proved most valuable to the political leaders of Islam well after his disappearance from the scene.

Ibn Sina, the spiritual successor of al-Farabi, comes dangerously close to the Judaeo-Christian notion of an intermediary between God and man when he suggests, in the tradition of the Shi'ites, that the role of caliph, who is indispensable to the distribution of justice within the state, is that of a "vicegerent" of God on earth! This approaches heresy in the traditionalist's sense of the oneness and singularity of God and his relationship to every human person. This notion is a logical extension of the psychological model of human personality devised by Plato. The idea is later seriously contested.

The creative ingenuity of the Islamic scholars during this time of transition is astounding. That they were willing, even eager, to employ and explore the Greek philosophical system and manipulate it and modify it and adapt it to fit the Islamic understanding of man and the world is both fascinating and admirable. Ibn Rushd, though at odds with many Muslim philosophers, was keen to employ the Platonic understanding of the human person. The human soul, said he, was comprised of the rational, the irascible, and the concupiscent, and these, in terms, corresponded to the fundamental virtues of wisdom, courage, and temperance. The confluence of these does not, however, bring about true happiness but only a coupling of the contemplative life with the life of act intelligence. This is the unique Islamic contribution to the Platonic notion of human happiness. The contemplative life is not sufficient for a believing, practicing Muslim. The Muslim of faith must also be actively involved with his mind and his deeds for only therein can true fulfillment be found for only in doing so is God to be served. Service to God is the ultimate expression of happiness and fulfillment in this life with the promise of the life to come.

The supreme virtue of justice, says Ibn Miskawayh, comes from God Himself and it comes by way of submission to the holy law. Justice must be rendered in the world to all people everywhere as an expression of worshipful obedience to the will of God Himself.

Al'Ghazali, the quintessential philosopher and ethicist, builds boldly upon the psychological model of Plato in his construction of an Islamic mystical worldview. For al'Ghazali, happiness is the highest good and can be achieved in the form of worldly good or otherworldly good. The latter is the highest for it is our ultimate goal in life in service to God. However, otherworldly good cannot be achieve alone, it must be accompanied by and nurtured by worldly good -- the four fundamental virtues of wisdom, courage, temperance, and justice. When combined with the bodily virtues, external virtues, and divine virtues, these converge in the life of the servant of God to create the final virtue which is "divine support," nurturance from God for the virtue embodied in the life of the servant believer. The great mystic, al'Ghazali, recites the path to fulfillment. It is found in the life of the faithful servant on his search for God. Seeking after God is the highest calling of all and must conform to two guiding principles, namely, the seeker must always be governed by the "divine law" of God, and the seeker must hold the search for God perpetually in his heart. To obey the law of God and to forever seek after Him is the true road to fulfillment. The passion of human love, for the Sufi's, is the analogy for this quest for God and here Islam meets up with the Jewish mystical tradition of the Hassids and the Christian mysticism of the medieval Carmelites.

ETHICAL THEISM AND TRANSCENDENT AUTHORITY

As radically divergent as ethical theism is in its Judaic, Christian, and Islamic expressions and formulations, the overarching affirmation in all three traditions is that ethical authority is derived from a transcendent source, namely God. That Catholics and Protestants different in their understanding of the relationship between the Church (*magisterium*) and Scripture (*Sola Scriptura*) does not alter the fact that ethical authority derives from the God of the Bible for all Christians. Though Judaism is content to embrace a doctrine of God which includes a repertoire of anthropocentric behavior, there is never a doubt that all authority resides in the Creator of Heaven and Earth. For Muslims, their radical monotheism is relentless in its claim for the total and uncompromising authority of God alone. That ethics is a derivative of Divine Being itself, there is no doubt among Jews, Christians, or Muslims. *Morality as the right thing to do exists because God says it!*

CHAPTER TWO

ETHICAL HUMANISM
in the Thought of Sir Julian Huxley

Ethical Humanism defines ethics as coming from within the human experience, an "internal" code of behavior. Ethics is what is prescribed by human experience. Morality is doing the right things because of human reason. Moral behavior is doing the right things because it is the right thing to do for people.

> "For my own part, the sense of spiritual relief
> which comes from rejecting the idea of God
> as a supernatural being is enormous."
> --Sir Julian Huxley
> *Religion Without Revelation* (1957)

Since we cannot cover all humanistic thought given its expansiveness from the 18th century onwards, I will address the school of thought most closely aligned to religion, or, at least the humanistic school most willing to explore a relationship with religious philosophy, namely, that of the work of Sir Julian Huxley. Whereas ethical theism requires an ethic, ethical humanism implies one. Monotheism is to religion what humanism is to ethics -- it is the core of the thought system. Humanism can no more function without ethics than monotheism can without religion. Since we have chosen to explore the humanism of Julian Huxley as an exemplar, indeed, the quintessential proponent of religious humanism, we will in this discussion speak of religion-as-ethics, that is, religion as the purveyor of ethics. Since humanism is devoid of an interventionist God-concept, the ethics being espoused by humanists will not be Bible-centered nor divinely derived. Rather, ethical humanism draws from the human experience as the arena for ethical formulations and not from an ethical system revealed by a divine source.

Our purpose here, then, is to explore the nature of ethics as defined and developed in the humanistic tradition wherein there is no biblical concept of God but there is, however, a concept of morality. Here, we will explore the concept of religious humanism with special reference to Julian Huxley. Of particular interest is the prospects of a "non-theistic spirituality," or, a spirituality "in the absence of God." The *presuppositional apologetics* school of hermeneutics suggests that "all argumentation with presupposition is circular," thus, so long as we define our terms carefully and with self-consciously articulated presuppositions, we should end up proving ourselves to be right. This is the case with religious fundamentalists, so why shouldn't it be the case with rational scientifically-minded humanists as well? We will explore, then, the possible meaning of the words "religion" and its sometimes companion "ethics" when they do not imply a "personal" God and we will also explore the range of definitions of "God" which might allow for a post-biblical religion and a non-biblical god. Why bother?, it might be asked, and that will be another challenge in this discussion. To demonstrate that the use of "religious" language in a "godless" world may or may not make sense.

By beginning with a biographical sketch of Sir Julian Huxley, this will allow for the setting up of the perimeters around the concepts of "religion," "ethics," "humanism," and "God." We will employ the use of the Princeton anthropologist Clifford Geertz's classic behavioral science definition of religion as it interfaces with Huxley's definition. Then, we will explore Huxley's definition of the "connectedness of all reality" as a humanistic ally contrived definition of "God." The intention is to maintain dialogue with the faith-based crowd without losing faith with the scientific and scholarly community.

As we have already said, the point to be made here is that all argumentation with presupposition is circular. So, once we have set up our operational definitions of such terms as "religion," "humanism," and "God" to our own satisfaction, there is no reason why we might not explore, then, the viability of a religion without God and a religion based upon the operations of the universe as understood through scientific inquiry. While resisting the Catholic tendency to "baptize" Huxley by means of Karl Rahner's notion of the "anonymous Christian" or Thomas Aquinas' notion of the "baptism of desire," we might still demonstrate the viability of a religion without revelation. The connectedness of all reality implies a union of all phenomenal existence and in response to this reality, the human community will inevitably encounter fundamental religious experiences such as awe, wonder, and reverence when presented with the profundity of the universal process of evolution. We will argue that awe, wonder, and reverence are not solely the dominion of believers in a transcendent God but constitute an experience intrinsic to the human person when confronted with profoundly moving and emotionally charged realities -- not just a God of miracles and magic, but a universe infused with complexity. If we can hang on to a sense of transcendence without the biblical baggage, we might be able to move on towards a "religious humanism" which embraces both humanistic values and awe-inspiring experiences fostered by an evolving universe. The emphasis will be upon the unitive reality of humanism rather than the dualistic idealism of biblical theism.

Our interest here, rather than a biographical study of Huxley's life and work, is to explore the impact of his thought upon modern day humanism and its relationship to traditional religious thought. Huxley became early, owing to the influence of his grandfather and the family ethos, interested in the critique of religion from a scientific perspective. He was a close associate of the British rationalist and humanist movements and was an Honorary Associate of the Rationalist Press Association from 1927 until his death in 1975. He was actively involved in the formation of the British Humanist Association and in 1963 became its first President. He was also the first President of the International Humanist and Ethical Union in the United Kingdom and before the 1965 national conference, he spoke of the need for "a religiously and socially effective system of humanism." Huxley truly believed that humanism could serve as a "replacement religion," a religion "without divine intervention or supernatural revelation."

In a famous treatise, Huxley(1941) wrote: "What the sciences discover about the natural world and about the origins, nature and destiny of man is the truth for religion. There is no other kind of valid knowledge. This natural knowledge, organized and applied to human fulfillment, is the basis of the new and permanent religion," ending the treatise with the optimistic concept of "Transhumanism," i.e., "man remaining man, but transcending himself by realizing new possibilities of and for his human nature." In 1961, he gathered around him the best twenty-five minds in the world of science and humanism and produced a major address on this general theme, entitled, *The Humanist Frame,* in which he concluded that "the increase of knowledge is driving us towards the radically new type of idea-system which I have called Evolutionary Humanism ... Humanism is seminal. We must learn what it means, then disseminate Humanist ideas, and finally inject them where possible into practical affairs as a guiding framework for policy and action." No true insight into the meaning and nature of evolution and its impact upon human understanding is worth the effort without the further aggressive application of that understanding to public policy.

Huxley wrote several major works in the continuing tradition and influence of his grandfather in the field of rationalism and humanism, including his three most internationally acclaimed books entitled, *Religion Without Revelation* (1927), *The Uniqueness of Man (*1941), and *The Humanist Frame* (1962). His cryptic observations about modern western thought dismiss traditional, historical, and non-western notions of supernatural forces operative in the universe to which we hold tenaciously and irrationally. Huxley said in his little classic, *Religion Without Revelation:* " We are used to discounting the river-gods and dryads of the Greeks as poetical fancies, and even the chief figures in the classical Pantheon -- Venus, Minerva, Mars, and the rest -- as allegories. But, forgetting that they once carried as much sanctity as our saints and divinities, we refrain from applying the same reasoning to our own objects of worship." In his once famous but now mostly forgotten Conway Memorial lecture, he said:

> The solution ... would seem to lie in dismantling the theistic edifice, which will no longer bear the weight of the universe as enlarged by recent science, and

attempting to find new outlets for the religious spirit. God, in any but a purely philosophical -- and one is almost tempted to say Pickwickian -- sense, turns out to be a product of the human mind. As an independent or unitary being active in the affairs of the universe, he does not exist. (*Science, Religion and Human Nature*, 1930).

Huxley's concern centered upon the certitude which commonly characterizes the religious position with respect to reality, faith-based absolutism which defies rational defense or explanation. "Any belief in supernatural creators, rulers, or influencers of natural or human process," he explains, "introduces an irreparable split into the universe, and prevents us from grasping its real unity." This duality introduced and perpetrated by a spirituality of matter and spirit, characterizes the religious worldview which then inevitably fosters a mindset of dualism which divides reality. Huxley's interest was based upon biological science and evolutionary understanding of the emergence of the world such that monism, a unitive reality, rather than dualism, a binary reality, is the basis of all existence. "Any belief in Absolutes, whether the absolute validity of moral commandments, of authority of revelation, of inner certitudes, or of divine inspiration, erects a formidable barrier against progress and the responsibility of improvement, moral, rational, and religious."

It can be argued that Huxley was a far more insightful and forward looking thinker than is generally recognized these days even, sad to say, among humanists themselves. Though humanism has been around since the Enlightenment in some form or another, Huxley elevated the humanist's contribution by integrating modern scientific understanding with biological evolution. Not alone in this situation, Huxley has too quickly and unfairly been overlooked and forgotten even within communities of scholarship which both owe him much and have yet much to learn from him. A major contributor to the education of the public regarding evolutionary biology and breakthroughs in genetics and the potential contribution to public policy such understanding can have, his long-term legacy to the modern scene has to do with his insightful integration of science and policy. He was, in many respects, a solitary figure in breaking ground regarding such things as the significance of evolutionary theory in physics, engineering, cognitive psychology, and biology. By calling attention to the biological concept of "emergence" within an evolutionary worldview, he pointed to the mutual influence in quantitative change and qualitative transition, leading to such concepts as interactive feedback systems. A pioneer in considering the nature of "cultural and social evolution" within a biological understanding of emergent life systems, Huxley called attention early on to the inevitability of human behavior -- cultural, social, political -- transforming the evolutionary process operative within the ecosystem of the earth. Harvard's Edward O. Wilson, whom we will discuss later, and Oxford's Richard Dawkins, have both paid such tribute.

Huxley's mother, Julia (for whom he was named) was, interestingly enough, one of Lewis Carroll's favorite photograph subjects as a little girl living in Oxford. After her first child died, Julian was born and became a special focus of motherly attention. She founded a school for girls after her marriage to Julian's father and even after her early death at age forty-six, the school continued to thrive. She had a deep sense of religion, he explains in his autobiographical reminiscences(1970), "not orthodox Christianity, but rather," he says, "a pantheistic trust in the essential goodness of the universe coupled with a sense of wonder." Interestingly enough and in spite of his mother's early influence upon him

41

regarding these sensibilities, it was, he says in his recollections, "my aunt Mary Ward's book, *Robert Elsmere,* that made a deep impression on me, and helped to convert me to what I must call a religious humanism, but without belief in any personal God." Like his grandfather, Thomas Henry Huxley (1825-1895), Julian found the notion of a "revealed religion" literally "incredible," says Ronald Clark in his biography of the Huxleys. Clark quotes Julian as saying that "on the basis of our knowledge of history and comparative religion, I am convinced that the idea of a god as a supernatural but somehow personal being, capable of influencing nature and human life, is an hypothesis which has been set up to account for various awe-inspiring and mysterious phenomena in man's experience which do not seem to have any natural explanation." This notion of religion as an answer to the inexorable quandaries of life we will address in our exploration of the work of Clifford Geertz later in this discussion.

Huxley became convinced, following the lead of his grandfather but pressing on with the newly emerging insights of advancing biological research, that, "from inanimate matter, through animate matter to the fully conscious mind," Huxley anticipates the work of Teilhard de Chardin, for whose now famous book, *The Phenomenon of Man,* Huxley himself wrote the Preface in which he said that "Evolution had continued, with man and his attempts to erect an ethical structure merely one of the steps in an evolving process." This is where Huxley saw the direction for research and the maturing of the post-biblical mind of modern science going. Though usually avoiding labels, he did find himself occasionally using the term "evolutionary humanist" as an acceptable self-characterization when called upon to do so. He pushed for modern science to assume responsibility for the future by embracing a "faith in the vast and as yet almost untapped resources of human nature." He said, "I use the word 'Humanist' to mean someone who believes that man is just as much a natural phenomenon as an animal or a plant: that his body, mind and soul were not supernaturally created but are all products of evolution, and that he is not under the control or guidance of any supernatural being or beings, but has to rely on himself and his own powers."

We are, in a Sartrian sense, "condemned to freedom," and, therefore, through "no merit of our own, have become responsible for the entire future of ourselves and the planet we inhabit..." Therefore, if man is to assume the leadership of the evolutionary process operative within the universe, we must erect an "ethical structure which will help us realize our great potentialities." We cannot count on some outside, supernaturally revealed, source for this help. If help comes, it comes from the human community. It comes from within ourselves.

The agenda for Huxley and, he believed, for all responsible scientists, was a unity of knowledge informed by science and systematized by reason. Since the only truly viable universal knowledge is scientific, by which he meant knowledge based upon verified observation or experimentation, it stands to reason that this unitive knowledge can only be fostered by the intentional abandonment of pseudo-systematizations of knowledge found in myth, magic, and superstitious worldviews developed and perpetrated by religious and ideological institutions. This unity of knowledge based upon sound scientific principles must be established upon five fundamental principles (*adapted from the* Humanists *website*):

> (1) the unity of nature, as opposed to all forms of dualism; (2) all nature as process, to be explained by evolution rather than any static mechanism; (3) evolution as directional, but only in the sense that it

generates greater variety, complexity and specificity of organization -- even though this may often lead into dead-ends; (4) evolutionary advance as defined in terms of the realization of new possibilities in nature; and (5) an evolutionary view of human destiny, with humankind recognized as the chief instrument of further evolution, as against all theological, magical, fatalistic or hedonistic views of destiny.

Huxley's passionate pursuit of a world of united knowledge built upon the solid foundation of evolutionary science mobilized for the further development of our understanding of the universe was ever present in his writings. The term used most often and early in his work was "scientific humanism," a term defined ironically by a biblical phrase. "One sentence, to my mind," he said, really contains them all -- "to have life, and to have it more abundantly." His main contention, throughout his long productive literary life, was that within the worldview of scientific humanism, the human community must be fully and completely responsible for planning and guiding the continuous evolution of the universe. Not relying upon a supernatural power or intervening God, it is within our own capability and accountability, to ourselves and to the world, that we must rely. There is a strong Sartrian sense here of our ultimate freedom to control our own destiny and, by extension, the destiny of the entire universe.

Huxley had little patience with a childlike yearning for a supernatural being who sees after everything, intervenes helter-skelter according to the petitions of persons and the whims of fancy. It is within, not without, the universe that the answer to the meaning and purpose of life is to be found. "I am not merely agnostic on this subject," he explained when speaking of his grandfather's own position regarding a supernatural personal being, "I disbelieve in a personal God in any sense in which the phrase is ordinarily used. ... God is the creation of man." Furthermore, he wrote, "It is impossible for me to believe in God as a person, a ruler...Supernaturalism and revealed religion are dead, because they are meaningless....there is no longer need or room for the supernatural."

Facing a burgeoning fundamentalism which America specifically and the West generally were becoming increasingly subjected to, Huxley was determined to confront this retrograde mentality with a counterbalancing scientific worldview. This he intended to do by offering up evolutionary humanism as a modern religion, a religion based on scientific knowledge and intrinsically materialistic rather than other-worldly and spiritualistic. He felt that the rational and informed strata of society would be empowered to implement the findings of scientific research for the betterment of humanity if they were systematically instructed in the implications of evolution. And religion, the driving force within the human community, as a meaning-system, could enable that implementation if constructed upon this worldly reality rather than other-worldly spiritualism. Rather than based upon the interventionist God of the religious fundamentalists, rational human beings could base their religion upon a meaning-system derived from an evolutionary understanding of the emergent universe. This kind of religion Huxley called a "new idea-system" in his 1961 collection of essays entitled, *The Humanist Frame.* Huxley wrote:

> This new idea-system, whose birth we of the mid-twentieth century are witnessing, I shall simply call Humanism, because it can only be based on our understanding of man and his relations with the rest of his environment. It must be focused on man as an organism, though one with unique properties. It must

45

be organized round the facts and ideas of evolution, taking account of the discovery that man is part of a comprehensive evolutionary process, and cannot avoid playing a decisive role in it.

The uniqueness of Huxley's appeal lay not with his emphasis upon the priority of human interests and concerns *vis-à-vis* other life forms within the non-rational world. The unity of knowledge Huxley saw took for granted as valuable the stratification of life forms. His emphasis, the profound uniqueness of his insight at this juncture in human history and scientific advancement, had to do with his assertion that human consciousness itself was both a manifestation of evolutionary processes and has a rightful place at the head of an emergent development within the universe. Humankind is not only an indispensable component of life within the universe, we are the "top most leaf of evolution," we are the universe come to self-awareness. *Humanity is the consciousness of the world.* And, though we are part and parcel of the universe, we bring with us "unique properties," namely, consciousness and self-reflective awareness thereby empowering the universe to think.

In other places, Huxley called this more formally "evolutionary humanism," in an effort to distance his humanism somewhat from the traditionalists' understanding of 19th century humanism which was static and certainly not susceptible to Huxley's notion of the profound impact evolutionary science should have upon our understanding of the nature and destiny of humankind. Even the outspoken proponents of evolution in the previous century, under the leadership of Thomas Henry Huxley, never presumed to integrate Darwinian evolution into the biology classrooms of the university and public schools of England. The risks, it was feared, were too high, both professionally and personally, to press the issue of Darwin's possible impact upon the scientific understanding of human behavior.

A book such as mine, *Naturally Good: A Behavioral History of Moral Development* (2005), could not have been published or even imagined without the work of Spencer, Darwin, and the Huxleys. Timothy J. Madigan, in an article appearing in 2002 in the *American Humanist*, entitled "Evolutionary Humanism Revisited: The Continuing Relevance of Julian Huxley," went so far as to say that "for a long period of time even such agnostics and humanists as the philosopher Bertrand Russell (1872-1970) shied away from exploring the implications of evolution for the future of the human species, let alone address how it had led to the contemporary members of the species." Understandably, the 19th century humanist within the academy has suffered unfairly for being lumped into a social Darwinism with the likes of Herbert Spencer, the social philosophy long and falsely charged with philosophical inhumanity as related to social policy. Spencer never intended to discount natural human compassion nor did the 19th century humanists intend to disassociate completely from the biological insights of Darwin. But it happened, and the price paid then and now has been great.

Huxley, on the other hand, has re-entered the discussion, fearless of criticism from his own scientific community and daring in his assault upon the religious fundamentalists. Believing that "religion" was imbedded in the human heart such that it was intrinsic rather than externally derived, Huxley proposed the outlandish idea of re-defining religion in this-worldly terms, in humanistic and scientific terms devoid of superstition, magic, and the much touted transcendent interventionist God, who is subject to the prayers of the faithful and vengeful to the point of barbarism upon those who refuse to believe. Huxley said a resounding "NO" to such a religion and to such a God. Religion, he believed, could be, since it is most decidedly a human construct, reconstructed using the ingredients of a scientific knowledge of the world and extricated from the shamanic and totemistic superstitions of a pre-rational mind. As a meaning-system and idea-system, it can be based upon a conscious understanding of the workings of the universe, a grasp of the nature and function of evolution itself as the focal point of awe, wonder, and reverence without the necessity of a super naturalistic intrusion of irrationality. Madigan explains Huxley's rationale this way: "Religions, like other cultural artifacts, are created by humans to answer basic needs....The desire for mystical transcendence is simply the deeply felt thirst for knowledge ... but previous religions had become static, too concerned with preserving dogmas and rituals, and were no longer in tune with the new scientific understanding of evolution that had revolutionized such fields as geology, biology, physics, paleontology, and cosmology."

It was believed by Huxley that the ingredients of religion -- awe, wonder, reverence -- could be found within the world of humanity, therefore, not needing to go outside. Going outside the world is what ancient prehistoric and pre-modern people did in an attempt to answer the mysteries of life -- Where did we come from? Who are we? Where are we going? Why do good things happen to bad people? Why do bad things happen to good people and a thousand other inexorably and intractably difficult questions. With modern science instructed by evolutionary theory, we understand these things more clearly and rationally. The Unknowable is now relegated to the as yet merely but only temporarily Unknown! As science chips away at our ignorance, the Unknowable continues to shrink. And, explains Herbert Spencer, if there is a God, he seems to be unknowable, and, therefore, outside the realm of human inquiry and human discussion. If there is a God, he has failed in making himself quite decidedly known to humankind in any consistently clear fashion. And if the sacred books of religion are the books of God, he has also failed in making clear what his message is, but rather has given mixed messages, often at odds with each other, thereby fostering centuries of hostility, hatred, and war. One would think that a God who could create the universe would be somewhat more gifted at making his will rather clearly known. As it is, religious people are left to their own devices in deciphering their own sacred books, all confusing, all contradicting, all illusive in terms of a unified Divine message. Just think of the energy expended among Christians over the past centuries trying to get together themselves, to say nothing of getting together with other religions. If there is a Divine message, it is indecipherable and, thus, Spencer is right again, it inevitably falls outside the Knowable and, thus, does not concern humanity.

With Huxley and those of kindred hearts, the challenge to humanity which constitutes our "most glorious opportunity, is to promote the maximum fulfillment of the evolutionary process on this earth; and this includes the fullest realization of our own inherent possibilities." Rather than "letting go and letting God," whatever that might mean to a rational mind awaiting intervention from a transcendent God, why not own the world from whence we have come and take our rightful place of leadership? The consciousness of the universe resides in the human mind and, therefore, a rational mandate would be to use it, not abandon it to a magico-religious outside agitator! The religious mind, at the end of the day, would have us abandon our rightful duty to continue to develop and refine an ethic worthy of the name. Rather than looking to external revelations -- tablets, books, prophets, saints -- ethical humanism calls upon us to look inside ourselves, inside the world processes embodied in evolution. It is easier, we have seen proven time and time again, to read the book of nature, to decipher the DNA code, than to understand the so-called sacred books of God. The nature of the scientific enterprise, experimentation, testing, retesting, new experimentation, etc., leads to understanding where the religious enterprise of textual analysis, interpretation, argumentation, sectarianism, etc., all seem to lead to more hatred, fear, and war.

Huxley explained in his 1964 collection of essays entitled, *Essays of a Humanist*, precisely what he intends by the concept of evolutionary humanism.

> Man is not merely the latest dominant type produced by evolution, but its sole active agent on earth. His destiny is to be responsible for the whole future of the evolutionary process on this planet ... This is the gist and core of Evolutionary Humanism, the new organization of ideas and potential action now emerging from the present revolution of thought, and destined, I prophesy with confidence, to become the dominant idea-system of the new phase of psychosocial evolution.

Regrettably, Huxley's optimistic prediction has not only not come to pass but, alas, a quiet, surprisingly disturbing turn of events has seen the rise of religious fundamentalism in a variety of traditions and with a heat and passion never anticipated. And if the irrationalism of such religious fanatics was not enough, many of them, under the guise of "scientific creationists," have marched upon the scene proclaiming the biblical creation story to be scientifically true! At a time in the world of science when we are on the brink of incredibly heartwarming breakthroughs in medical research in this country and abroad, our public schools find themselves being held hostage by the religious fanatics of an interventionist God. It has been suggested that the rational mind is under siege from the primitive-minded religionists to a greater extent than even during the time of Darwin. The denial of evolutionary science today in America -- in schools, in churches, in social policy -- is stifling at every level and in every corner of the country. Any sustained effort at moving forward with scientific research is constantly in jeopardy.

One of the ironies of the "intelligent design" people is the fact that even if one would concede an argument for God from the "intelligent design" point of view, that does not move them any closer to the God of the Bible! The distance from intelligent design to the Christian God is even greater than the distance from agnosticism to theism. For it is too clear to be denied that the intelligent design folks are really interested in "bringing the world to Jesus," and not to the God of the philosopher or engineer, not to God as a Watch Maker but to God as an incarnate being in the person of Jesus of Nazareth. If they would come clean, if they would really and truly be honest with the rest of us, we could at least see where they are really coming from and not hiding under the false umbrella of an intelligent source of the universe. The evolutionary humanists can, quite decidedly, accept the notion of intelligent design by claiming evolution itself as the intelligence embodied in the human mind and the design is the systematic sustaining of creation through evolutionary processes of survival and adaptation. But no, the intelligent designers will not allow human intellect and evolutionary adaptation to answer the intelligent design challenge for they must bring in their doctrine of the fall, original sin, redemption, salvation, and an eternal abode with God. What baggage for the rational mind to worry with handling!

That Huxley is no prophet is too clearly indicated by Madigan's summation of the failure of humanism to displace religious fanaticism: "The humanist approach has not become dominant, and a scientific exploration and understanding of the universe has come into heavy criticism

51

not only from fundamentalists but also from the so-called 'postmodern' school of thought, which tends to see science as merely another -- and not necessarily superior -- ideology." And, if that were not enough, scientific humanists of the *not too inclined to accommodate religionists orientation*, have found Huxley's thought less than easily palatable. The criticism is not with the idea-system but with the propensity to employ religious nomenclature, viz., sacred, reverence, etc., when it is not necessary (science has its own vocabulary, thank you very much) but also too easily misunderstood to the point of bordering on deceptive. When Huxley uses the word "sacred" he does not imply, as do the theists, a transcendent God but rather a human reverence of mind for the beauty and grandeur of the universe as it has evolved under its own efforts without the aid of an intervening power source called God. Why bother? is the legitimate question of Huxley's own scientific crowd who would much prefer to employ the language of science to enhance and embellish a scientific explanation of the universe.

Here we are exploring Huxley's position with respect both to his anticipated demise of the Christian religion and to the eventual rise of a secular religious understanding of the universe, called here a "new religion," or, as I have chosen to call it, a "post-biblical" religion of ethical humanism. "It is certainly a fact," says Huxley, "that Christianity does not, and I would add cannot, satisfy an increasing number of people and it does not and cannot do so because it is a particular brand of religion, which is no longer related or relevant to the facts of existence as revealed by the march of events or the growth of knowledge." Huxley suggests that increasingly the rational mind is having to play tricks on itself to stay in the religious wagon. When, with every passing day, we continue to learn more about the origins of the universe, how it has evolved, how the human mind is developing, all of this scientific advancement in rational explanations of the universe has systematically chipped away at the pre-modern worldview of an ideological system developed in a flat magical world fraught with superstition. In order to maintain any semblance of integrity, the rational mind is being forced to choose between an interventionist notion of an outside power source *called God* or an intrinsic model of emergent life based upon internal processes *called evolution.*

In an attempt to blaze a humanistic path between positivism and functionalism, the late Clifford Geertz of Princeton's Institute for Advanced Studies has put forth what is increasingly being considered the most useful definition of religion to-date in the social sciences and serves well the agenda of Huxley also. "The view of man as a symbolizing, conceptualizing, meaning-seeking animal opens a whole new approach to the analysis of religion," says Geertz (1966). While attempting to demonstrate the legitimate perimeters of the social sciences, and especially anthropology, in analyzing religious phenomena, Geertz conscientiously withholds any challenge to the methodological credibility of the history and phenomenology of religions in their pursuit of the essence of religious experience. He has put forth the following definition: "Religion is (1) a system of symbols which acts to (2) establish powerful, persuasive, and long-lasting models and motivations in men by (3) formulating conceptions of a general order of existence and (4) clothing these conceptions with such an aura of factuality that (5) the moods and motivations seem uniquely realistic."

As did Huxley earlier, Geertz suggests that a fundamental characteristic of religion is the address to the "problem of meaning"—meaning suggesting purpose and direction to life and meaninglessness suggesting chaos and pointless existence. "There are at least three points," says Geertz, "where chaos—a tumult of events which lack not just interpretation but interpretability—threatens to break in upon man at the limits of his analytic capacities, at the limits of his powers of endurance, and at the limits of his moral insight. Bafflement, suffering, and a sense of intractable ethical paradox are all radical challenges with which any religion, however 'primitive,' which hopes to persist must attempt somehow to cope." Without doing violence to the social scientific perspective of Geertz, we can say that religion constitutes an experientially motivated address to the problem of impending chaos in the existential experience of humankind. Furthermore, we can say that beyond, behind, or under religion's capacity to cope with bafflement, suffering, and inextricable ethical paradox lies the "essence of meaning" to which these expressions in quest of existential meaning are enduring witnesses.

This implied extension cannot, of course, be pursued in this study, but I have considered it at length in another place in my book, *"In the Beginning..." The Paleolithic Origins of Religious Consciousness* where I refined Geertz's definition as follows: *Religion is (1) a complex of behaviors and ideologies (2) consisting of rituals and myths (3) which appeals to a transcendent legitimacy (4) embodying a worldview and ethos (5) addressing the verities of life and existence and (6) conveying a dynamic level of psycho/social reality (7) which is self-validating to the individual and community.*

Geertz is not oblivious to this possible extension and logical elaboration of his position, nor is he antipathetic to such an endeavor. "The Problem of Meaning in each of its intergrading aspects," continues Geertz, "is a matter of affirming, or at least recognizing, the inescapability of ignorance, pain, and injustice on the human plane while simultaneously denying that these irrationalities are characteristic of the world as a while." He goes on to say,

"The existence of bafflement, pain and moral paradox—of the Problem of Meaning—is one of the things that drive men toward belief in gods, devils, spirits, totemic principles, or the spiritual efficacy of cannibalism, but it is not the basis upon which those beliefs rest, but rather their most important field of application." This *drive toward belief* is conveyed through cultural symbols and bespeaks man's quest for meaning, for an existential meaning which challenges chaos and which pursues order. "Whatever else religion may be," Geertz says, "it is in part an attempt (of an implicit and directly felt rather than explicit and consciously thought-about sort) to conserve the fund of general meanings in terms of which each individual interprets his experience and organizes his conduct...."

While the symbolic anthropologist Geertz has provided us with a definition of the meaning and nature of religion, its function, its origin, its purpose and direction, Huxley had in the previous generation ventured into the discussion himself in an attempt to both scope out the fundamental perimeters of religion's purpose and function and then to identify within scientific humanism those same fundamentals. "A Religion," he explains, "is an organ of man in society which helps him to cope with the problems of nature and his destiny -- his place and role in the universe. It always involves the sense of sacredness or mystery and of participation in a continuing enterprise; it is always concerned with the problem of good and evil and with what transcends the individual self and the immediate and present facts of every day." We have already seen the leading anthropologist of the century, Clifford Geertz, defining religion precisely so, pointing out that religion "functions" to assist in explaining the unexplainables of life such as personal tragedy, natural disasters, etc. If by mystery (or "sacredness" which is Huxley's synonym), one means confronting the "unknown" or the "unknowable," then religion need not automatically and inevitably imply a transcendent power source, a God standing outside the universal creation intervening whimsically or upon petition by those engaged in manipulative prayer vigils. Furthermore, one does not necessarily have to assume that the problem of right and wrong is only solved by "revealed" truth through the medium of sacred books, priests, divine revelation, etc. In my book, *Naturally Good: A Behavioral History of Moral Development,* it was demonstrated rather conclusively that moral behavior has evolved directly through the human community's growing consciousness of survival behavior rather than from tables of stone or books rained down from above or transmitted magically to a holy man.

But, in addition to addressing the intractable nature of human experience when faced with the verities of life as well as the profound social and personal issues of right and wrong, religion also carries with it a system of thought. Or, more precisely, religion evolves a systematization of experiential reflection upon the encounter with the *mysterium tremendum et fascinans* (tremendous and fascinating mystery) which, in higher religious systems, is called theology. "A religion," Huxley says, "always has some framework of beliefs, some code of ethics, and some system of expression -- what are usually called a theology, a morality, and a ritual." This systematization of experience leads to a theologizing enterprise usually appropriated by those placed in positions of power related to their capacity to tease out from the experience an "internally logical" explanation for the questions of life. Thus, we see the emergence of the shaman, the priest, the prophet. It has been suggested by some anthropologists that the priesthood, not prostitution, is the oldest profession. Be that as it may, the theological agenda grips the religious community by systematizing the faith experience into a code of morality and a creed of beliefs which then, in turn, become the criteria for judging membership within the community as well as those outside the experience.

Of course, we see already that the fundamental ingredients needed to make a religion are also found within the scientific and humanistic community as well. There is a fundamental encounter with the life experiences within the human community seeking explanation and a concerted effort on the part of the more reflective members of that community to systematize the inquiry into the nature and meaning of the experience in question. This is done with a sense of reverence for the mystery yet to be revealed and those specifically involved in the systematization of the inquiry are held in special regard by the community. Scientists and science function not unlike priests and theology in this process. The difference, the profoundly fundamental difference, is that whereas the scientific community will only accept rational inquiry and deduction based upon rigorously enforced rules of investigation, the religious community relies upon the systematizers and interpreters of the faith experience based upon their knowledge of the transcendent power source, the intervening God of the universe, who stands above and outside reason and logic.

All theistic religions are supported by this theological framework which centers upon the basic belief "in the supernatural and the existence of a god or gods, supernatural beings endowed with properties of knowing, feeling, and willing akin to those of a human personality." With Christianity, however, this supernatural God, "who at a definite date -- until recently specified as 4004 B.C. by the bishops of the Church -- created the world and humankind in essentially the same form in which we appear today; a creator capable of producing miracles and of influencing

57

natural events, including events in human minds, and conversely of being influenced by man's prayers and responding to them." Up until and in many ways even after Darwin, Bishops Ussher, Calmet, and Hales' dating of the moment of creation of the world by the God of the Bible was held as firm and true, and is still held with all of its irrationality among many fundamentalist churches even today.

The Christian community, summarizes Huxley in his now famous proposal for a "new religion of ethical humanism," embraces a plethora of beliefs which today's modern scientific mind finds irrational, irresponsible, and demeaning to the integrity of the human person and the human spirit. He gives a splendid litany of these beliefs such as the notion of a last judgment at an unspecified time in the future at which time the earth will be destroyed, eternal life after death with punishments and rewards based on a notion of salvation through a belief in Jesus of Nazareth as the Son of God, an earthly resurrection of the body, the raising of the dead Jesus, only the Christian belief is true and all others are lost ("No other name under heaven is given among men whereby we must be saved" says the Christian Scriptures), the coming of Jesus on a cloud to judge and condemn or save every person who has ever lived (fetuses constitute a slight problem here but not considered by Christians insurmountable), and so on.

"Christianity," says Huxley, "is dogmatic, dualistic, and essentially geocentric ... based on a vision of reality which sees the universe as static, short-lived, small, and ruled by a supernatural being." Based on the creative and rigorous labors of thousands of scientists -- physicists, chemists, biologists, psychologists, anthropologists, archeologists, historians, and humanists -- this traditionalist religious worldview, says Huxley, "is incommensurable" with it. For the scientific and rational community, "our picture of reality becomes unitary, temporally and spatially of almost inconceivable vastness, dynamic, and constantly transforming itself through the operation of its own inherent properties." No room exists in this worldview for a transcendent intervening power source. This "new religion" has as its worldview a vision based solidly and squarely upon the reality of evolution, an evolutionary process which is intrinsic to every component of its composition.

Rather than try to show how these two views of reality can be related -- they cannot and he is quite explicit about that impossibility -- Huxley attempts to characterize this new view of reality through the employment of religious language redefined in light of evolutionary science. He does this by systematically sketching a picture of this "new vision" of reality. In light of this scientifically informed worldview, "all reality is in a perfectly valid sense one universal process of evolution," he explains. This evolutionary process consists of three components, viz., (1) the inorganic or cosmic, occurring with the physical and chemical interactions which have produced the solar systems and galaxies of the universe over the past six billion years; (2) evidential but rare occurrences of self-reproduction based upon the principles of survival and natural selection producing a myriad of complex variations of increasingly higher organizational forms of life from microscopic organisms to humankind; and (3) in the last stages of evolutionary development during the past one million years or so, within the matrix of this self-reproducing complexification process, neurological acceleration has occurred within the human brain producing consciousness, a self-reflective awareness capable of rational, sequential, logical thought processes grasping and imagining spirals of complexity fraught with potential and utility.

The final stage, that of the emergence of the human

mind, is where we are today and where our future lies for tomorrow. The workings of psychosocial evolution, the development of language, art, music, literature, political processes, and domestic socialization have all occurred within the last few thousand years but are, without question, accelerating exponentially in response to the application of the human community's intentionality with respect to survival and improvement. Following on the slow-moving stages of typological development -- from microscopic organisms to vertebrates to fish, amphibians and reptiles, from reptiles to mammals, and finally to *homo sapiens* -- humankind is the crowning apex of this evolutionary process.

Early in our evolution, the human community answered questions regarding the intractable difficulties of life through magic and fantasy, through mythological beings and superstitious fears. As we accelerated in our systematization of this reflection, we produced religious ideas which produced a meaning-system of symbols, myths, and rituals designed to calm fears and appease the troubled mind demanding answers to the riddle of life. Through it all emerged a God made in our own image who would respond to laments for help, protection, and nurture, a God who would punish the disobedient (of the rules articulated and enforced by his priestly representatives) and reward the obedient (those following the rules mandated by the divinely appointed enforcers of the sacred codes which had been received and recorded). "However," Huxley says in concluding this overview, "with the development of human science and learning, this universal or absolute God becomes removed further and further back from phenomena and any control of them. As interpreted by the more desperately *liberal* brands of Christianity today, he appears to the humanist as little more than the smile of a cosmic Cheshire Cat, but one which is irreversibly disappearing."

That is not to say, however, that the basis of this sense of the sacred, this sense of the "divine," is likewise and summarily expunged from the human experience when once we are freed from the magico-superstition of a God of power and might, ruling the universe by whim and fancy as it suits Him. On the contrary, this sense of the sacred, what Huxley calls the "stuff of divinity," is intrinsic to the human experience, the experience of awe, wonder, and reverence in the face of the evolutionary creation of the universe. Whereas volcanic eruptions, thunder, hurricanes, sexual reproduction, birth, disease, and death all were once the causes of this awe and wonder in the face of danger, the modern community of scientific understanding knows the nature of these phenomena. Yet, we are still gripped with awe, wonder, and reverence when we encounter the splendidly complex realities of the emerging universe, the discoveries of the solar system, DNA, and radiation. These and many other scientifically discovered realities capture our sense of awe and wonder today the way thunder and lightning, volcanic eruptions and floods did our ancestors centuries and millennia ago. In this fashion, the humanist is allowed to speak of the divine, not as a transcendent reality but as an intrinsic reality of the universe itself.

Furthermore, to the extent that we can imagine a "religion of evolutionary humanism," it is a religion not based upon supernatural revelation from an external God but rather a revelation that "science and learning have given us about man and the universe." This is revelation, humanly facilitated revelation, revelation based upon scientific research and intellectual effort. The revelation of an external super power intervening periodically and erratically in the affairs of humanity has now been displaced by a revelation based upon scientific inquiry and research methodology, a human agenda seeking a humanly created mechanism for revelation inside this world, not of another and yet to be encounter hereafter world. For the humanist, there is an unrelenting belief that "man is not alien to nature, but a part of nature," says Huxley. By moving to the humanist worldview, we move away from archaic dualism to a scientific unity of knowledge. There is nothing excluded in the humanist's world for all things are a result of the evolutionary process and must be accounted for and not dismissed as unworthy, unacceptable, or merely unusable.

Furthermore, the ethical humanist is not only "a product of the universal process of evolution, but capable of affecting the process which has produced him, and of affecting it either for good or ill." It is human destiny, determined by the evolutionary process from the beginning, that we have the capacity to direct our future and the future of the universe. Being the mind of the universe, the thinking envelope of the earth (in the words of Teilhard de Chardin), it lies within us to determine the direction of our future and, as we have already seen in our very short history, this can be for either the uplifting or the tearing down of humanity and the earth. We have the choice. It is our responsibility. The power lives within us and not outside of us. It is internal to the human experience of reality rather than external. There is no "letting go and letting God," for we hold the knowledge of the power source of evolution and must then use it for the survival and advancement of humanity and the world. We are the product of the universal process of evolution and now this product, the human mind, must assert its rightful place of leadership in moving the universe to ever higher realms of complexity and refinement. This leadership will not be, cannot be, by sheer force of power derived from our understanding of the process. Rather, leadership must be in concert with the evolutionary principles of universal emergence. We must partner, we must collaborate, we must cooperate with these principles, using them, directing them, but never abusing them, in the pursuit of an increasing potential for a better life for humanity and the world. It is an ecological system of collaboration rather than a theocentric system of externally derived domination.

A hallmark of this new humanistic religion, a religion based upon this world rather than another, will have the "task of redefining the categories of good and evil in terms of fulfillment and of desirable or undesirable realizations of potentiality, and setting up new targets for its morality to aim at." Since ethics is a human construct, humanity must engage in its codification and organic transformation, always in response to a deepening understanding of the universe and our place in it. We are no longer left to consult a book of rules. Rather, the evolutionary process must become the source consulted when determining the ethical future of human relationships to each other and to the universe. This process, says Huxley, "will assign a high value to the increase of scientifically based knowledge; for it is on knowledge and its applications that anything which can properly be called human advance or progress depends." The fundamental difference between a supernaturally driven ethics and that of ethical humanism is that the focus for the latter is on this world, this moment, here and now, and not on the "sweet bye and bye," "the hereafter," or the "life after death," of the traditionalist religions. Boldly and with a determined courage, humanity will embrace its own destiny and that of the world and will own the responsibility, not waiting on a God to come and take us away from it all, but relying upon our rightful place here and the necessity of caring for it and fostering its advancement into higher realms of consciousness. Huxley's concluding remarks are worth reprinting here for all to hear and enjoy:

Humanism also differs from all super-naturalist

religions in centering its long-term aims not on the next world but on this one. One of its tenets is that this world and the life in it can be improved, and that it is our duty to try to improve it, socially, culturally, and politically. The humanist goal must therefore be, not Technocracy, nor Theocracy, not the omnipotent and authoritarian State, nor the Welfare State, nor the Consumption Economy, but the fulfillment Society. By this I mean a society organized in such a way as to give the greatest number of people the fullest opportunities of realizing their potentialities -- of achievement and enjoyment, morality and community. It will do so by providing opportunities for education, for adventure and achievement, for cooperating in worthwhile projects, for meditation and withdrawal, for self-development and unselfish action.

"The sense of spiritual relief which comes from rejecting the idea of God as a superhuman being is enormous." These words from Huxley's little classic, *Religion Without Revelation*, states rather clearly from where Huxley and the ethical humanists are coming. It should be clear by now that Huxley and his followers are not suggesting that there is no religion, no spirituality; rather, they simply contend that spirituality and religious consciousness need not have its source and origins from outside the universe, from an intervening transcendent power source. Surely we have demonstrated already that awe, wonder, and reverence are fundamental ingredients in the human experience and need not derive their reality from an afterlife or heaven or a God who stands outside of creation. Religious behavior and spiritual awareness are endemic to the human fabric of our consciousness as they embody our fundamental sense of fascination with the world and all reality.

But, for Huxley and the humanists, there is a genuine sense of relief, of a sigh of contentment and respite from anxiety, fear, and pressure from a superhuman personalized God who created the world, destroyed it because of his anger, sent His son demanding that His son die in order to appease His anger, and then threatening everyone with an eternal fire of physical punishment if they did not obey His law even when to determine exactly what that law is seems very problematic. Huxley suggests that the enormity of this sense of relief is not in embracing atheism as a way of living and perceiving but of being exonerated from a primitive notion of a spiritual super-being which exercises jurisdiction over the universe and the individual! Not that we then are at liberty to be merely secular and devoid of any sense of spirituality; on the contrary, this experience of relief is decidedly spiritual in the sense that we are freed and empowered to explore and cultivate our own indigenous spirituality, informed by modern science and mature reason devoid of nursery rhyme superstitions and magical images of a primitive cosmology.

This *natural spirituality*, one might call it, grows out of a liberating consciousness of the demise of the tribal God of supernatural transcendence and grows into the self-reflective awareness of the unity of the cosmos wherein there is no separation of mind and matter, body and spirit, sacred and secular. Rather, there is the realization that, in light of the revelations of evolutionary biology, the universe is a oneness of creation, a unitary reality, a monolithic entity *vis a vis a vis* the dualism of an archaic theology of divisibility -- God versus humankind, mind versus matter, body versus spirit. To realize and embrace this cosmic discovery that there is no separate supernatural realm but that all phenomena are part and parcel of the same natural process called evolution brings on this "sense of spiritual relief."

Humankind is a central, maybe the central, player in

this evolving universe. The biblical God can hardly be a predictable player because, as He is portrayed in biblical mythology, He is sometimes in the world and sometimes out of it, coming and going as whim and fancy move him. Humanity is fully a partner and participant in the evolutionary process, the thinking envelope of the universe and, therefore, responsible for the oversight of its destiny. Reason and rational thought fly in the face of a belief in a supernatural being coming and going, in and out, here and gone, setting rules in a variety of conflicting and contradictory forms and media such that no two groupings of human persons can agree as to exactly what this God has said and to whom and when. Every religion that counts on this intervening power source is set for conflict, suspicion, fear, and, yes, often hatred of other religions who, likewise, believe they have heard or received the words of God, labeling themselves differently from other faith communities. There is no end to the madness once the hypothesis is accepted that this intervening God has in some fashion or another "revealed" His "will" to humankind.

Both the human community and the human person are the key players in the riddle of the universe. A product of three billion years of evolution, it is within the consciousness of the human person that this evolutionary process has become "self-aware." Therefore, whether we like it or not, we are ourselves responsible for the continual evolving of the planet. In spite of this new cosmic consciousness, the human community tends to clutch by-gone systems of comfort in the face of uncertainty. Even when modern science has demonstrated the tribal and superstitious nature of God-centered religion's disenfranchisement from the facts of evolution, we tend to hold on to it as a small child clutches the blanket with which it has slept in hopes that it will continue to offer comfort even when it no longer covers the child from the cold and the uncertainties of daily life. In the absence or perceived absence of a really viable alternative cosmology and worldview to traditional theism, many times those sensing the void in their lives continue to rearrange the chairs on the Titanic in the full or dim awareness that the ship is going down in spite of all efforts to the contrary.

However, this radical evolutionary crisis of accelerating consciousness through which humankind is presently passing can only be surmounted by an equally radical reorganization of our dominant system of thought and belief. We must move away from the tribalism of a supernatural deity to a scientifically justified awareness of the oneness of the universe and our pivotal role in its on-going development. There is a courage required here, a mature courage of both personal acceptance of the centrality of the evolutionary process in the universe rather than that of our own individual personhood as well as a courage which must assert itself in seeking to foster a pan-psychosocial commitment to the emerging universe. Therefore, I am personally important and we are collectively important in cosmic terms, in terms of our indispensable role in the embracing and nurturing of this unitary process within the cosmos.

And there is room, indeed, a necessity, for religion, a religion of the future, a religion constructed out of the materials of this new consciousness and not out of the discarded relics of supernaturalism and dualistic formulations of primitive cosmologies and worldviews. Religion, certainly, is a human construction, a necessarily created ideology which provides answers to life's bafflements, inexorable injustices, and intractable mysteries. Religion functions universally as a mechanism for dealing with the problems and verities of life -- Who are we? Where have we come from? Where are we going? What are we to do?

Beyond Divine Intervention

Religion's three-pillared construction consists of (1) an intellectual or ideological framework (called theology), (2) a moral code of behavior (called ethics), and (3) a shared symbolic expression of wonder and awe (called ritual). And religion has been and is forced to either keep stride with socio-cultural and psychological advancements in communal understanding of the answers to these fundamental questions of life or decline in its effectiveness as the "answering mechanism" in the face of bafflement and quandary, exigencies and chaos.

If we are correct in our assessment of the present spiritual character of modern society, then western religion in its three-tiered monotheistic formulation is facing a devolution of viability. Rather, modern science has essentially disenfranchised western religions (Christianity, Judaism, and Islam) from their pre-scientific cosmologies with their accompanying archaic worldviews of supernaturalism and divine interventionism, thus leaving these religious ideologies in a holding position of protectionism and entrenchment. Because these traditional religious systems were constructed during pre-scientific times, their cosmologies and worldviews are out of touch with the common knowledge of historical information available to any school child. "Today," says Huxley, "the God hypothesis has ceased to be scientifically tenable, has lost its explanatory value, and is becoming an intellectual and moral burden to our thought." But, contrary to the misplaced fears of traditionalists, this deep sense of relief brought on by the abandonment of the God-centered universe does not usher in an era of rampant immorality and individual or social irresponsibility. Nevertheless, what must occur is the conscious creation of a cosmology and worldview supported by an ideology, a morality, and a symbolic system worthy of the new consciousness of the oneness of the universe. *We need a religion which matches our science!*

The necessity for this new religion is due fundamentally to the human awareness of and need to respond to the cosmic reality of the divine within nature, what ethical humanists are calling here "natural religion" (*religio naturalis*) or "natural spirituality" (*spiritualitas naturalis).* The source of this new cosmology and worldview, this evolution-centered rather than god-centered religion, is the universal human sense of "the divine," the very same experiential phenomena which produced tribal religions in the first place. Supernaturalism is not an indispensable ingredient of religion but rather merely an early and naïve human formulation expressive of an awareness of "the stuff of divinity." "The Gods were constructed," says Huxley, "to interpret man's experiences of this quality," i.e., this stuff of divinity, for the word "divine" does not originally imply the existence of gods but rather testifies to the existence of the experience of the *mysterium tremendum et fascinans*, the fascinating and tremendous mystery of the meaning and mystery of life infused, as it is, with awe, wonder, and reverence. The gods of old were created to objectify the social experience of both need for authority and source of authority in matters related to the answering of questions concerning bafflement and inexorable tragedies of life.

The "divine" in human experience, then, may be defined as that which the individual person and human society perceive and define as worthy of adoration, that which elicits awe and wonder. Divinity might be thought of as that raw experiential material of composite experience of individuals and societies out of which religion grows or is created. A humanistic religion, a religion based on the science of evolution and fostered by the awe and wonder perceived and adored in the creation of the cosmos by the human community, invites conscious development as we invite and work to foster ever deepening appreciation of nature and music and art within our offspring. Religion can be grown, developed, fostered, the same way other levels of heightened consciousness can be. It need not be based upon a pre-rationalistic notion of a supernatural being infused with super powers of intervention. A humanistic religion may very well be intentionally grown from the materials of mathematics, biology and psychology as well as art, music, and literature instilled with the wonder, awe, and reverence induced from a genuine encounter with scientific knowledge and the created world.

By embracing evolutionary biology as the source of all things, this humanistic religion can proceed with the fundamental hypothesis of growth and development, fulfillment and achievement, as the purpose and direction of its function within society and for each individual. Because human potentialities constitute the world's greatest resource, as yet only barely grasped, then by tapping and directing these vast resources of human possibility, the religion of the future has at its disposal the full participation of the consciousness of the universe, human consciousness, in pursuit of ever greater senses of personal and social fulfillment and achievement. The resulting moral codes and symbolic rituals will necessarily have to be created out of the combined energy and experience of those involved in developing the ideological framework of this *humanistic religion of evolutionary consciousness.*

For example, in place of any notion of personal eternity, this effort will direct itself to a sense of enduring process. A sense of personal salvation will be replaced with the notion of a continuing development of a deepening sense of commitment to and responsibility for the physical environment of the world and the psychological environment of the human personality. Salvation will then mean an

John H. Morgan

investment by the human community in the perpetuity of the world rather than a personally enduring self. Salvation may imply survival but not for the person but for the cosmos. The Christian's casual disregard for the longevity of the world's existence owing to a fundamental belief that when Jesus returns the world will be destroyed (thus implying that God himself has only a passing interest in the earth), the humanist is unequivocally committed to the perpetual endurance of the world for its own sake and the sake of all life here on it. This is pure Julian Huxley and the message is clear and sound. No petitionary prayers to a supernatural and intervening being, an external power source, will be thought relevant or rational, but adoration and aspiration will characterize the self-reflective meditations of the human person and society. Thru self-examination and socially tutored psychological exploration, individuals and societies will identify and foster mechanisms for the purpose of deepening the sense of responsibility and fulfillment.

Of course, the more jaded and crusty secular humanists among us marvel at the bother. It might be argued, and somewhat persuasively, that the bother is not worth the results for the humanists already know what they know and the religious community is certain of its own position. It certainly could be argued, as was said early in this discussion, that "all argumentation with presupposition is circular," and, thus, the humanists end where they started and likewise do the faithful. To employ traditionally sacrosanct nomenclature such as "religion," "God," "divinity," "awe," "reverence," "wonder," and the like while providing each one with a somewhat different meaning not only does not move dialogue ahead but seems dangerously close to actually contributing to its ineffectiveness. If we can't agree on the meaning of the words we use, then how can we ever come to an understanding, to say nothing of an agreement, on these issues?

Still and all, the warm-blooded humanists who so desperately desire to free religiously trapped persons from their shackles can hardly resist proposing the use of the old language with new meaning, or, more precisely, with a deeper and more reflective understanding of our present reality. For those who experience deeply awe, wonder, and reverence in the world about them, in themselves, and in their encounters with others, the yearning for a validation of that experience is real and legitimate. Yet, many of these same individuals find themselves disenfranchised from the religious establishment for refusing to embrace a pre-modern notion of an interventionist God, a God of the Bible, who consistently exhibits primitive and irrational behavior. The Garden of Eden, the flood, parting of water and stopping the sun, blood sacrifice of the son to appease the anger of the father God, the virgin birth of a God/Man, an eternal damnation by fire -- all of these things fly in the face of reason and modern science. However, the experience of awe, wonder, and reverence still persist, even grow, in the midst of a deepening understanding of the evolutionary process of creation. Isn't there a legitimate place for such as these in the world?

ETHICAL HUMANISM AND ANTHROPCENTRIC PRIMACY

The source of the ethical code in ethical theism is clear -- God says it and Man must do it. Whether Muslim, Christian, or Jew, the divine revelation of humanity's relationship to God -- however conceived and nuanced within and between the three monotheistic religions -- is epitomized in the transcendentally revealed code of ethics. People do the right thing because God says to do it. Ethical humanism is, on the other hand, based upon Julian Huxley's famous declaration of independence from God -- "...the sense of spiritual relief which comes from rejecting the idea of God as a supernatural being is enormous" -- boldly declaring freedom from any divine revelation and rather celebrating a humanly created ethics, an ethics based upon the human experience of what is right and wrong. Moral behavior is not revealed by an interventionist Being (the outside agitator) but by thoughtful, rational, and compassionate people. Ethics is the codification of what works within the human experience. *Morality as the right thing to do exists because the human community makes it so, that is, morality exists because Man says so. It is the act of human will rather than of Divine Will.*

CHAPTER THREE

ETHICAL NATURALISM
in the Thought of E. O. Wilson

Ethical Naturalism defines ethics as coming from within the cosmos As an internally generated code of behavior. Ethics is what is prescribed by the world (natural environment). Morality is doing the right things because it is best for the world. Moral behavior is doing the right things because it is the right thing to do for the world.

E(dward) O(sborne) Wilson was born June 10, 1929, in Birmingham, Alabama, and is an entomologist and biologist known for his work on evolution and sociobiology and, by some, is called the "father of biodiversity." A childhood accident claimed the sight in his right eye and later, in adolescence, he lost part of his hearing. He struggled with math and a mild form of dyslexia. The accident with the eye, he suggests amusingly, probably pushed him into the study of ants which he could bring up close to his one good eye for careful scrutiny. After earning both a B.A and M.A. from the University of Alabama, he received his Ph.D. from Harvard University and is now a world renowned entomologist, in particular the use of pheromones for communication among ants. Today, Wilson is the Pellegrino University Research Professor Emeritus at Harvard University today and an Honorary Fellow of the Graduate Theological Foundation from which he holds the Doctor of Humane Letters. Hailed as "the new Darwin" by Thomas Wolfe, and one of "America's 25 Most Influential People" by *Time Magazine*, he has twice received the Pulitzer Prize. He is also famous for starting the sociobiology debate when he wrote his now highly acclaimed *Sociobiology: The New Synthesis* (1975), an enormous volume comprised of 697 extra-sized pages. Wilson sought to extend the understanding he had gained of the principles of the intricate behaviors of social instincts to vertebrate animals. Prior to this landmark tome, he had published *The Insect Societies* (1971).

His inquiries into the new science called "sociobiology" argues that social animals, including humans, behave largely according to rules written in their very genes. The theory sparked controversy because it not only appeared to contradict cherished beliefs about free will, but also, according to critics, harked back to retrograde ideologies charging that some human groups were biologically superior to others. He and his colleagues have over the years defended and refined sociobiology such that at this point it is now a dictionary word. Of this new discipline and the resulting book he says: "It was a new discipline that I was proposing, which was the scientific study of social behavior in all kinds of organisms on a foundation of biology. It was a very successful attempt in the study of animal behavior. It succeeded immediately. But I also decided to apply it to that special species of animal, Homo sapiens, and when I did, I just suggested that maybe there were some implications of this for human beings as well....I said that maybe there is such a thing as instinct and human nature and maybe this is the way to study it, with this new discipline. And in the middle seventies that was not an idea permitted in most of the social sciences on American campuses."

A third book, entitled, *On Human Nature* (1978), is concerned with the further extension of these same principles to the human species. Not intending to alienate the philosophical community, Wilson nevertheless and necessarily must challenge their age-old reflective methodologies, especially since they seem consistently not to have employed an evolutionary perspective regarding human moral behavior. With scientific evidence testifying so convincingly that moral behavior is directly linked to biogenic brain function and the inevitability of those functions producing a survival-based moral code of ethics, philosophers along with everyone else must ultimately come to face the reality that consulting the personal human emotional responses to moral challenges is hardly either scientific or responsible. Since morality has evolved from an instinctual response to the necessity of speciel survival, then discussions of ethics and morals must have an evolutionary and biological foundation.

Wilson is profoundly aware of the actual "human" dynamic of moral decision-making and that it lies with the human person and the human community to determined, rationally and without any sense of an outside spiritual force, what should and should not be done, what is right and wrong, what is good or evil. It lies with the human community to make the determination, based upon the biogenically-derived moral censors, just "how human we wish to remain!" The human community cannot, like the ethical theists, presume to "let go and let God" for, in the absence of any outside source of moral conduct, it is we ourselves who must decide what to do and the basis upon which that decision is made must consult and be informed by the biological foundations of our own moral behavior.

Here Wilson has made his historic call for an "integrated" science of human nature dependant upon the natural sciences, social sciences, and the humanities. But this new integrated science of human nature must be "scientific" rather than philosophically reflective and consultative with those who claim a source of knowledge and wisdom outside the realm of human reason! He says a "guru" can't help us nor can politicians making decisions about scientific matters of which they know little or nothing. Because we and the cosmos are faced with the inevitabilities of evolutionary process, we must, therefore, consult the evolutionary sciences in order to have real factual information relevant for the making of sound decisions which will affect the future of the world, and of humanity itself. Only ethical naturalism can embody the natural and social sciences in the ethical formulations of moral decisions. Ideologies and faith-based pontifications become not only irrelevant but dangerous.

While being generous in attributing to Kohlberg a serious contribution to the understanding of moral development among children of the human species, Wilson is fully aware that Kohlberg, of course, has based his work upon the monumental work of Jean Piaget. Wilson is eager to demonstrate that when the social and behavioral sciences base their findings upon empirically demonstrable scientific studies, the biological community is ready to embrace those findings. What isn't allowed is a faith-based science which begins with doctrine and ends in apologetics.

The brilliance of Wilson's agenda is reflected here in his explication of the role of biology and its efforts to circumscribe and articulate the physical components of ethical decision-making. Going beyond philosophical speculations, biology through its "neurophysiologic and phylogenic reconstructions of the mind" has set for itself the scientific study of the generative work of the mind in evolving "an enduring code of moral values." Though the social sciences will be radically reoriented, Wilson believes their role in the human sciences will eventually be elevated rather than demoted.

In my own work, entitled, *Naturally Good: A Behavioral History of Moral Development from Charles Darwin to E. O. Wilson*, I have attempted to address this problem and commenced the work by quoting a statement from Darwin in his *Descent of Man*: "...as far as I know, no one has approached it (moral development) exclusively from the side of natural history." This is precisely what Wilson is now doing by calling attention to the reality of genetic evolution to moral development. With Darwin, Wilson contends that a biological understanding of the origins of human moral behavior will actually enrich and deepen our moral behavior and ethical formulations. If we understand the biological origins of our decision-making powers and processes in determining right and wrong, then our decisions can be more rationally based and less linked to outside interventionist ethics which are based upon dogmatic ideologies derived from mythological cosmologies of ancient, pre-scientific origins.

Wilson's *The Diversity of Life* (1992), which brought together knowledge of the magnitude of biodiversity and the threats to it, had a major public impact, and still today he continues entomological and environmental research at Harvard's Museum of Comparative Zoology. However, *Consilience: The Unity of Knowledge* (1998), has proven to be the bombshell it was predicted to be. Here he draws together the sciences, humanities, and the arts into a broad study of human knowledge. His premise in this controversial book is that a common body of inherent principles underlies the entire human endeavor. Again, following the controversies of his work in sociobiology, his "consilience" work has again placed him at the center of debate and controversy.

"The gist of this book," says Wilson, "is that, contrary to the widespread views coming out of what's called postmodernism, truth is relative, each discipline, each person is a little universe unto itself. Contrary to that -- and it still ha strong influence on many campuses today -- we really can unify knowledge. Science has done it from physics all the way to biology of the mind and ecology, by cause and effect relationships, and it's time now the book argued to look into the possibility that we can take that network of explanations, that unity of knowledge, on into the social sciences and even into the arts." One of the main reasons for writing this book, he explains, is to bring about a convergence of environmentalists working with philosophers on the major ethical issues affecting the world and the human community. Environmentalism, according to Wilson, is the convergence particularly of the study of the environment with the ethical issues which surround it. Here, then, of course, is the obvious justification for the development of an ethical school of thought called "ethical naturalism."

The word itself was coined in the last century and refers to long-separated fields of inquiry that come together and create new insights. For instance, the marriage of chemistry and genetics this past century created the powerful new science of molecular biology, the basis of genetic engineering. The controversy surrounds Wilson's belief that all human endeavor, from religious feelings to financial markets to fine arts, is ripe for explaining by hard science. Philosophers and artists, to say nothing of theologians and religious leaders, bristle at what Wilson calls his "unification agenda," his attempt to show, as he puts it, that "the greatest enterprise of the mind has always been and always will be the attempted linkage of science and the humanities."

"I believe that the Enlightenment thinkers of the 17th

and 18th centuries got it mostly right the first time," he says. They assumed a lawful, perfectible material world in which knowledge is unified across the sciences and the humanities. Wilson calls this common groundwork of explanation that crosses all the great branches of learning "consilience," and he argues that we can indeed explain everything in the world through an understanding of a handful of natural laws. The world he envisions is a material world that is organized by laws of physics and evolves according to the laws of evolution.

Wilson makes his point by means of a fascinating tour through the Enlightenment and the age of scientific specialization. Among his topics of interest are "professional atomization," which works against the unification of knowledge, and cultural relativism, that is, "what counts most in the long haul of history is seminality, not sentiment," he says with amusement. In examining how a few underlying physical principles can explain everything from the birth of stars to the workings of social institutions, he offers fresh insight into what it means to be human.

Determined to keep the argument squarely on target regarding the origins of ethics and moral behavior, Wilson doesn't allow the speculative thinkers to embrace a domain assumption without calling it what it is, namely, human surmising. The scientific community is going to insist upon clarity of choice -- either the ethical code is God given or man made. Either the ethical code which the human community employs to govern our moral behavior has its origins "outside" of the cosmos from an intervening source or it comes from "inside" the cosmos from a source intrinsic to the evolutionary process. Either a theology of ethics from God or a biology of ethics from the cosmos -- one must choose for both can't be operative simultaneously. The appeal to "natural law," according to ethical naturalism, is

John H. Morgan

fallacious for either it draws its validity from an interventionist deity, and thus is merely theologizing, or it draws its validity from the evolutionary process itself, something I have chosen elsewhere to call "systemic integrality," which, then, is biological. God made (ethical theism) or man made (ethical humanism) -- one must decide and the decision is based either on science in the latter instance or theological musings in the first. Later we will see Wilson move further into the cosmic validation by employing what I have chosen to call *ethical naturalism*, that is, calling upon the cosmos itself as the validating source of moral decision-making.

Wilson's genuine interest in mollifying and engaging the religious community in his quest to mobilize the human community in earth-saving endeavors is strengthened by his readiness not to dismiss theism outright. Of course, as a scientist, he must certainly dismiss any semblance of a fickled God who periodically, episodically, and erratically intervenes in the affairs of the world and of humanity. For most theists, this dismissal of a "personal" God makes conversation difficult if not impossible, Wilson is ready to concede that science is not now prepared to make an empirical argument against the possibility of a "cosmological God" who created the universe. And, he is not inclined to embrace the Huxley agenda of redefining religious nomenclature such that a creator God concept might simply mean the evolutionary process itself. Fundamentally, the issue of the human code of ethics and moral behavior still resides in the question as to whether or not moral conduct has been revealed by an intervening God or evolved from a self-generative biological process within the cosmos. This question is not at all compromised by Wilson's disinclination to embrace atheism or his willingness to concede the possibility of a deistic cosmic creator.

81

Beyond Divine Intervention

Wilson's major contribution to the interdisciplinary dialogue going on now within the behavioral and natural science communities is the direct results of his call for an "interlocking of causal explanation across disciplines," what he has called "consilience." The notion, timely but disappointingly still perceived by some in the retrograde backwaters of the social and behavioral sciences as radical, seems amazingly mundane and matter-of-fact. That the biological and social sciences should work together in the plotting of the human species emergence and place within the cosmos is, says he, to be the mandated agenda for the 21ˢᵗ century. And, though some of the perimetric boundary issues are still left to relativistic speculations, the scientific perimeters of the issues of moral behavior are so much more narrowly refined than those within the religious community which relies always upon an interventionist transcendentalism, as to make the scientific agenda so much more reasonably viable now than the religious.

At the end of the day, Wilson is keen to continually remind us of our biological origins. Humans came, not from heaven, but from the earth and are directly a product of the evolutionary process which, necessarily, links us directly and irretrievably with all living things in the cosmos. As social critique and social commentator, few are better than E. O. Wilson. And, his scientific pedigree only contributes to that high place maintained by him and his critical assessment of the present state of humanity in the world. There is presently, to no one's denial and to many's dismay, a major confrontation between the two worldviews of religion and science, between a "religious transcendentalism" and "scientific empiricism." That transcendentalism continues, after nearly two centuries, of maintaining the high ground in religious thought is amazing to some and baffling to others. That scientific empiricism has not become the standard rule of thumb in all daily activities and discussions is a total mystery to those immersed in scientific work and thought. The behavioral intricacies of ethics and religion, says Wilson, are sufficiently complex as to have not yet been deciphered by scientific analysis. Yet, both ethics and religion are quite decidedly more intricately involved in the evolutionary process of human development than the religious community has been willing to admit or acknowledge. Their denial of such dependence on the biologically evolving process of human emergence continues to exacerbate attempts at meaning dialogue between science and religion. In order to stay viable as a moral source, religion will be forced to seek out ways of creatively and positively incorporating scientific insight into its own work and mission. The use of "poetic forms" of integration of scientific fact with religious mythos will prove helpful if not central to that process. In the meantime and throughout the process, the religious exponents of an interventionist transcendence must count on continual and unrelenting scrutiny by the scientific community of the religious message of the traditionalists.

Wilson is not shy in pronouncing an eventual outcome of the competition between science and religion. Religion will recede into the archives of human history like the ancient mythologies of past cultures and the secularization process which is carried by scientific empiricism will continue to reveal to the human community its origins, its present status, and the prospects of its eventual future, a future, I might add, which will call upon the human community to relinquish its "primacy" and to embrace its "systemic integrality" with the rest of the created and evolving cosmos. In other words, leaving ethical theism behind and moving through and beyond ethical humanism to a fully developed ethical naturalism.

Wilson's books on sociobiology and human nature

gave rise to a storm of controversy that has somewhat abated as the evolutionary behavioral ideas as suggested by Wilson have gained more acceptance. Both within and beyond academic circles, it was inevitable that ideas that are effectively concerned with fundamental questions of human life: its meaning and its inherent dignity, would have the potential to be enormously controversial. In the first paragraph of his book on sociology, he states his view of life in quite unequivocal terms as follows: "In a Darwinian sense the organism does not live for itself. Its primary function is not even to reproduce other organisms; it reproduces genes, and it serves as their temporary carrier ... Samuel Butler's famous aphorism, that the children is only an egg's way of making another egg, has been modernized. The organism is only DNA's way of making more DNA." The overall message carried, namely, that various kinds of social behavior are genetically programmed into all species, including our own, and that this programming is particularly true of the social behavior human beings label "altruism," which Wilson defines as "self-destructive behavior performed for the benefit of others." People are animals, their behavior has evolved just like that of the animals, and our culture has a biological component, he announced.

Cultures need to accomplish certain things, says Wilson, if they are to survive at all. They must assure effective use of natural resources, for example, which might involve the learning of all sorts of territorial and aggressive behaviors. And they must assure a degree of cooperation, which might involve learning altruistic behaviors, rules for sharing resources and for other social relationships. And they must assure a continuation of the population, which might involve certain courtship and marital arrangements, nurturing behaviors, and so on.

Wilson has argued that the preservation of the gene,

rather than the individual, is the locus of evolution, a theme explored in more detail by Richard Dawkins' *The Selfish Gene*, of New College, Oxford, Sir Julian Huxley's old teaching grounds. Wilson has also studied the mass extinctions of the 20th century and their relationship to modern society. He explains: "Now when you cut a forest, an ancient forest in particular, you are not just removing a lot of big trees and a few birds fluttering around in the canopy. You are drastically imperiling a vast array of species within a few square miles of you. The number of these species may go to tens of thousands. May of them are still unknown to science, and science has not yet discovered the key role undoubtedly played in the maintenance of that ecosystem, as in the case of fungi, microorganisms, and many of the insects." He continues, "Let us get rid immediately of the notion that all you have to do is keep a little patch of the old growth somewhere, and then you can do whatever you want with the rest. That is a very dangerous and false notion."

Wilson inadvertently created one of the greatest scientific controversies of the late 20th century when he came up with the idea of sociobiology. Sociobiology suggests that animal, and by extension human, behavior can be studied using an evolutionary framework. Many critics accused Wilson of racism and he was even physically attached for his views. However, Wilson never intended to suggest that human nature was static and independent of the environment. Nor did he intend to apply a 'survival of the fittest' model on human society as had been true of social Darwinists in the 19th century. The controversy caused a great deal of personal grief for Wilson and many of his colleagues at Harvard, such as Stephen Jay Gould, were vehemently opposed to his ideas. Nevertheless and in view of his international vindication, he has received many awards for his work, including most notably the National medal of Science and twice the Pulitzer

85

Beyond Divine Intervention

Prize.

Most recently, his 2002 book, entitled, *The Future of Life*, offers a plan for saving earth's biological heritage and has received a great deal of acclaim as offering a way out of our present dilemma regarding the environment and our role in surviving within it. In this more recent presentation, he draws on his forty years of research to make a passionate and eloquent plea for a new approach to the management and protection of our eco-system. Marshalling arguments from science, economics, and ethics, he demonstrates that proper stewardship of the earth's bio-diversity is not an option. Rather, it is a necessity, and a choice we must make if life is going to continue to thrive on the earth.

In *The Future of* Life, Wilson talks about the bottleneck of over-population as it relates to the future of life on earth and suggests that this is what humanity is currently experience. "We all, or most all," he explains, "realize that humanity has pushed its population growth pretty close to the limit. We really are at risk of using up natural resources and developing shortages in them that will be extremely difficult to overcome, and yet we have this bright prospect down the line that humanity is not going to keep on growing much more in population, that it is likely, if we can use the United Nation's projections at this stage, to top out at perhaps nine to ten billion, fifty percent more people than exist today, and then begin to decline."

In our modern context, Wilson goes on to explain, "we've really lowered the death rate and where poor people around the world, all except those in absolute poverty, have access to medicine and social assistance and so on, so their children can survive. In the long haul of history, however, where the well-off, the dominant, elements in the society have co-existed with the poor and the subordinate, it turns out, it's just the result of studies of these types of societies that have been made, that even though the poor having a larger number of children per capita, the children aren't living as long because of their condition, and those who are wealthy and having a smaller number of children are actually producing more children into the next generation."

In view of this demographic configuration, the human community is under ever increasing pressure to push our technological capabilities to the limit. But the fact remains, says Wilson, "that with existing technology, you can show fairly reliably the figures have not been seriously challenged to my knowledge that in order for the whole world, the whole world population to live in American standards, we would need four more planet earths!" This cannot, of course, continue. At the end of the day, Wilson says, he likes to think of that phrase that was used so effectively by the late Abba Eban, during the 1967 War. "When all else fails, men turn to reason."

We now know that natural selection and the evolutionary process constitute the fundamental basis of all modern science and all responsible understanding of humankind's place in the cosmos. That the human species (and all species, for that matter) evolved through a process of genetic change and environmental necessity (natural selection and the survival of the fittest) disavows unequivocally the necessity or the viability of an intervening deity and certainly not a personal being with transcendent powers of creation. Such a deity may, says Wilson, be sought in the philosophical question of "where did it all begin?" but certainly not in the creation of the cosmos for that privilege of place is reserved strictly for evolution. Metaphor, imagery, poetry, and mythos may embellish the creation story of the bible, but they are to no avail when set alongside empirical science.

The great spiritual dilemma created by this fact of evolution is that the human species, like all other living forms, has no place to go. That is to say, this is it, our place and experience in the cosmos is where we are and what we are doing now. There is nothing awaiting us in the "after life." Death is all that follows in the after life. Yet, since this is it, this should really and truly be it, it should be our focus, our passion, or mission to serve the cosmic needs. That the human brain exists to promote the increase and endurance of the human genes means that the human brain is dedicated to speciel survival and progeneration. That process requires rational thought. The human community must not now only serve ourselves but must look to the cosmos, its own needs, in order to assure our own survival and its survival as well. We must become "less" anthropocentric and more cosmocentric if we are ourselves to survive as a species.

When Wilson speaks of a "new morality," he is speaking of an ethical code of moral conduct which calls for doing the right thing for the cosmos, not just for a single species of living things in the cosmos. In order to discover this new moral code of ethical behavior, the scientific community must set about to track the evolutionary history of the universe and each of its species, particularly the human species, for it is human action which can destroy or sustain the cosmos through the use of rational thought and the mobilization of the empirical sciences. Because the new morality must be recognized as a human construct, the human community will necessarily be confronted with a plethora of behavioral options based upon the biological composite of the human species.

Our first dilemma is that the human species "has no place to go." The second dilemma of the human species is that our "moral behavior evolved as instinct," it is a product of biological evolution. Therefore, we can expect the scientific community to search out and investigate the very origins and meaning of human values, the source of all ethical and, indeed, political pronouncements. The indictment of the philosophical and theological community, suggests Wilson, is that this community of scholars concentrates its attention upon the "consequences" rather than the "origins" of the human ethical code of moral behavior thereby bypassing the empirical sciences while favoring speculative musings of religious and philosophical orientation.

Unless the social sciences and the humanities, including theology and philosophy, are willing to acknowledge and embrace the empirical contributions the natural sciences have made, are making, and will continue to make in our understanding of the evolutionary origins of human value systems, the human community will not be able to arrive at an integrated understanding of what it means to be human. Our very core understanding of humanity is linked to our knowledge of and willingness to accept our biological mandate. If we are not willing to take full cognizance of our biological composition, we will never be able effectively to implement a rational decision-making process of determining our moral destiny.

The convergence of the natural and behavioral sciences, says Wilson, has already and will continue to offer the human community the best possible avenue to search for a sustainable and empirically-supportable humanity. This "scientific materialism" is our last great hope for arriving at an integrated sense of what it means to be human within a community of ethical codes and moral behaviors, codes and behaviors selected and perpetrated by the community itself following careful and systematic analysis of our biological needs, origin, and destiny.

Ever the naturalist, Wilson is always keen to remind us of our earthly origins, of our relatedness to the earth, of our kinship will all other species on the earth, both living and extinct alike. Failure to recognize and embrace enthusiastically this connectedness with the earth and its other living inhabitants has been the cause, granted often unwittingly, of much of the environmental problems and pending ecosystem crises we face today. An ethical naturalism, based upon the primacy of the earth's environmental needs rather than a code of behavior based upon either mandates from God or mandate from anthropocentrists, is what we must develop and embrace if the cosmos itself is to survive with the human community as one of its grateful inhabitants.

Wilson is reconciled to the power, be it irrational, of religious belief and acknowledges that, in spite of all the scientific community has done over the past two centuries to educate the general public, religion continues to have the upper hand, the overall control of large masses of the human species. Wilson approaches but comes short of despairing over the power of a mythic confluence of irrational cosmologies in the face of empirical science. The power of religion is demonstrated in the human species' ready willingness to embrace any religious ideology rather than face the realities of finitude.

The scientific agenda in the study of religion, of course, is to identify and describe those biological components of human behavior called "religious." Wilson is fully aware of the explosive nature of this agenda, socially and culturally, and equally aware of the "scientific" problematic imbedded in the inquiry as well. One of the most provocative of characteristics of religious behavior, of course, is that the human animal is the only animal known to us to have such behavior. It's not enough to merely quote the ancient divines who explain that the human animal is the only living thing in need of religion for, as they are eager to point out, we are the only animal that sins! Scientifically and particularly biologically, what interests us is the empirically demonstrative behavior called "religious" and we can find no parallel analogy in any other animal.

Wilson's suggestion of a "deep structure" analysis is quite indicative of his confidence in the biological sciences. The genetically motivated religious behavior must be gotten at through the laboratory research which has the capacity to cut through the "self-deception" of those professionals who propagate the religious ideology. Natural selection, he suggests, can be analyzed at three levels -- *ecclesiastical*, which includes the binding and bonding power of ritual which are devised by the religious leaders for the purpose of emotional captivity; ecological by which is meant the environment within which this kind of captivity is operative; and *genetic,* shifts where cultural evolution and populations are fluctuating.

Wilson's rather bold claim that genes have a role in the development of the learning process itself within human beings is applied here by suggesting that gene frequencies are altered by ecclesiastical selection. We are wired to be religious, apparently! The genes influencing religious behavior are thought to constrain behaviors and motivate behaviors. Behavior, he suggests, is influenced by interaction with other learned behaviors, all of which are influenced by genetic constructs. This reliance upon genetically motivated behavior suggests that religious constructs of behavior are genetically linked. We behave religiously, not because of the reality of the ideology but because of the strength of the genetic coding. Wilson is not suggesting that religion is true. Far from it. He is suggesting, however, that the genes which favor survival are functionally operative within any ideology which favors the endurance of the species, whether that ideology is true or not. The issue is survival and religious behavior that favors survival, say the continuity of cohesion of the group, will inevitably be incorporated into the genetic composition of the organism.

With the ethical naturalists, Wilson is arguing that religion is genetic in the sense that the survival behaviors which assure the endurance of the human species are genetic and religious behavior functions in that way by virtue of enhancing and nurturing the cohesion of the group's own internal identify. In my book, *"In the Beginning...":* *Paleolithic Origins of Religious Consciousness,* I defined religion as follows: "Religion is a complex of behaviors and ideologies consisting of rituals and myths which appeals to a transcendent legitimacy embodying a worldview and ethos addressing the verities of life and existence and conveying a dynamic level of psycho/social reality which is self-validating to the individual and community." Wilson has gone even further. Beyond my argument for the psycho-social origins of religious behavior, Wilson argues that genetics itself favors the fostering of religious behavior. Not that religion itself is actually true in terms of its dogma or code of beliefs but that religion functions as a component of speciel survival. And, this behavioral complex fostered by the will to survival inevitably creates institutional forms for its continuance in human society.

This argument of Wilson's favors my own psycho-social definition of religion. The creation of a world that seems so unequivocally real and indisputably extant constitutes the religious institutions' primary agenda. No one dare question its reality lest by doing so one question the actual meaning of life itself. As my definition of religion suggests, religion consists of rituals and myths which appeal to a transcendent legitimacy. This legitimacy is fostered by a genetic drift to self-survival and to question the transcendent legitimacy of religion is to question the very meaning of life. To question the religious basis of social commitment is to question the legitimacy of the community. The genetic composition of the individual precludes such a frontal attack upon the community whose function is to foster the bonding of its members around a worldview and ethos designed to assure allegiance to religious authority.

Ethical naturalism, as a system of thought, is keen to point out that "religious behavior" and "moral behavior" are not synonymous, and, whereas the religious tendency to worship a monotheistic god is prevalent among human beings, it is not, however, universal. What is universal is moral behavior, behavior requiring the exercise of doing the right thing because it is the right thing to do for the community rather than because God said do it.

Though aware of and sensitive to the psycho-social and cultural infrastructural composition of religious behavior, Wilson is true to his own science when he focuses upon the "psychobiological" origins and explanations of faith. A belief in God, or an intervening deity, is fundamentally characteristic of religious faith and exemplifies the essential dependence upon myth even in the modern world. Whether or not the human animal is genetically dependent upon myth to function socially is yet to be established or determined but that myth still functions as an essential ingredient in the affairs of human life is without question. Much work is yet to be done in this provocative field of thought and the expectation is that it will prove most productive in further understanding the biological nature of faith.

Religionists, says Wilson, are not bound to an ideology restricting their mobility in the explaining of their faith. If the Marxists are tied to the ideology of dialectical materialism, the religionists are free to roam the world using first this, then that, explanation of their faith-based understanding of the world without any particular restrictions on pragmatic utilitarianism. The use of the creation myth -- an intervening outside deity who creates the universe but is exempt from its rules -- is the last and great refuge for the religious mind for it defies logic and reason and yet cannot be dislodged due to the power of its mythic import. Even the integration of a shallow understanding of evolutionary biology with a traditionalist understanding of an intervening yet transcendent and illusive deity is possible with a religious thought system called "process theology" which, on the surface, sounds both scientific and religious but when, upon closer analysis, it is not scientific but employs a naïve scientism to compliment and flatter a traditionalist theology.

Wilson makes the somewhat problematic insinuation that scientific materialism is itself a "myth." Though the religious establishment will jump all over this as a self-indictment of credibility, one must understand that Wilson is using the term "myth" in its historic "mythopoeic" meaning, namely, the realization that first-cause arguments are not demonstrably provable. What the religious establishment fails to realize is that good science is always operating on propositional laws and developmental hypotheses unlike religion which operates strictly on "faith-based" convictions. Wilson argues persuasively that the evolutionary epic can be as captivating to human imagination, if not more so, than any religious myth and is, unlike religious mythology, based upon empirically demonstrable evidence of historical development. One does wonder if Wilson has not inadvertently opened himself and the biological sciences up for naïve and simplistic dismissal by the religious community for having used the term "myth" to describe what in modern science we take as an historical given. Yes, honesty and integrity will assuredly take the day in time.

The boldness of Wilson is both humbling and intimidating. His quest to "divert the power of religion" for humanistic and scientific purposes is admirable, especially since his desire is to mobilize this strength of religious passion for the purpose of addressing the present and future demands of the world, for its continuance, for the quality of the life it nurtures in the universe, and for the prospects of a scientifically understood universe. Without doubt, scientific naturalism (and, by implication, ethical naturalism) will eventually and inevitably win over its current chief competitor in the spinning of mythic cosmologies. But whereas religion, and the passion it mobilizes, will endure in some capacity, albeit without an interventionist deity shackled to it, theology as a discipline, Wilson surmises, will not be able to survive the onslaught of scientific evidence which is systematically dislodging and debunking much of that discipline's stock in trade. In the process of unpacking the biological origins of religious ideology and behavior, scientific naturalism will be fully aware of the difficulties in not having ready to hand an irrational but powerfully gripping mythology of individual immortality or a god-mandated rightful place for human beings in the world. This kind of mythic imperialism exercised for so many generations by religion, such that it now is genetic, is not available to modern science, and may not be anytime in the foreseeable future. The "mythic imperialism" of a religion which promises eternal life to individuals and provides a worldview mandated by the social grouping's own deity is a hard competitor, especially when modern science relies, not upon irrational passion but upon empirical demonstration.

Yet, Wilson is optimistic about the long-term future of human reason. If humanists and scientists can't rely on the emotional power of conversion and divine obedience to mobilize the human intellect, thereby precluding scientists becoming secular priests, they can imagine an agenda of directing and guiding that religious and mythic energy towards a more responsible and meaningful address to the problems confronting the human community and the cosmos in which we live. Here is where Wilson and the Dawkins crowd part company. The ethical naturalism of Wilson seeks to engage the religious community for help in addressing the major issues confronting the cosmos whereas Dawkins dismisses that community as necessarily dysfunctional by design and intent. I have argued elsewhere in my book on Huxley, In the *Absence of God: Religious Humanism as Spiritual Journey (with special reference to Julian Huxley)* that Huxley's desire to utilize, through re-definition, religious nomenclature could be of some value in this effort to mobilize religious people for a humanistic agenda.

We behavior as a result of genetic evolution and yet those behavioral options are themselves the product of natural selection processes. The human species has survives and continues to survive owing to the configurated genetic elements which make up our nature, a nature that is forever embracing, integrating, adopting and adapting our hormonal feedback into the existential inevitabilities of on-going life. Wilson's insightful genius is here most evident. His talk of a biology of ethics, thus the basis of our present discussion employing the title, *The Biology of Right and Wrong,* is based upon evolutionary biology's understanding of the moral code of behavior which has evolved within the human species as a necessary survival mechanism. Rather than revealed by a outside deity, the human moral code of conduct has evolved within the DNA of the species itself. And, says Wilson, the study of this phenomenon through the parallel efforts of evolutionary biology and cultural evolution, that is, both the behavioral and natural science communities working together, will produce great results in the near future regarding the fundamental biological origins of human moral behavior.

At this point, Wilson takes a giant step beyond the early work of Sir Julian Huxley whose efforts on the part of a naively contrived eugenics devoid of a substantive understanding of the genome led him into both uncharted and troublesome waters. Wilson suggests that a "democratically" devised eugenics awaits the humanistic and scientific community once we have sorted out the complexities of human heredity dictated by the genome enterprise. The elevation (without God) of human rights as a primary value is central to Wilson's scientific prognostications. His work suggests that human beings embrace and perpetrate human rights as a fundamental ingredient of our species because it serves well the individual and the group. We do the right thing because it is the right thing to do, for the individual and for the group, not because God said do it.

The pontificating tendencies of the religionists are balanced by the humble prognostications of E. O. Wilson. Human moral behavior has surely evolved due to a process of natural selection which served speciel survival. Yet, says Wilson, "genetic fitness" perpetrated by fundamentally utilitarian motives of individual, family, and group survival does not complete the story. Neurophysiology will eventually decipher the genetic code of moral conduct, allowing us not only to understand the primary factors dictated by biology but the secondary factors dictated by social and cultural history. Wilson's hope and claim is that the epic of cosmic evolution will one day reach a level of literary sophistication such that in the telling of the tale, the human animal will be stirred in the same emotive ways as we are now by religious myths which are rapidly becoming devoid of credibility due to scientific and historical research. To tell the evolutionary epic with imagination and creativity, while staying on track with the empirically demonstrable facts, can inculcate and nurture a spirit of awe, wonder, mystery, and reverence which will convey the energy needed for the human community to finally recognize and embrace

97

our connectedness to the cosmos. Ethical naturalism will be the inevitable code of moral conduct generated by such an eventuality.

The indictment of intellectuals within the social sciences and the humanities is stinging in Wilson's assessment of the present state of Western popular knowledge. Science, the physical and natural sciences, has yet to be embraced and embodied in the culture of industrialized nations all the while those nations and cultures exist primarily and fundamentally owing to the contributions of those sciences. The irony is palpable! Scientific naturalism is now demanding and dictating a redefinition of the social sciences and humanities owing to the empirically demonstrable fact that human nature and human behavior are being understood by the biological sciences in ways that now preclude the social sciences and humanities, particularly philosophical speculations, from continuing their work in the same old traditional manner. If and only when the social sciences embrace the findings of the physical and natural sciences, particularly neurobiology and sociobiology, will the social sciences be able to continue to contribute to a scientific understanding of the human species and its place within the cosmos. Until that time, the social sciences and humanities are destined to continue their mantra of ancient formulas based upon now debunked myths and legends.

Wilson is not one to ignore or deny the emotional power, even the psychological addiction, which the myths of religions, even those which have long been abandoned or redefined in an effort to salvage them from scientific invalidation. The promise of eternal life and national glorification which comes from the intervening deity is itself strong enough to continue the function of religious behavior long after the basis of the promise has been deciphered and exposed. When it comes to religious additions, the explanation of the dubious origins of its faith is not sufficient to dislodge it from the human emotional matrix of the social group. Wilson suggests that only when scientific naturalism is able to grasp and enrich human imagination with the story of the epic of cosmic and speciel evolution will science be able to compete with the dead and dying mythos of religious cosmologies.

For one who has spent a lifetime studying the works of the Huxleys, it does this author good to see Wilson himself acknowledge and own his relationship to Huxley's great humanistic work. Scientific humanism and scientific materialism converge, however, in the work of Wilson, a work which goes beyond the historical limitations of the Huxleys. Wilson's awareness of the biological complexities of human genetics itself has caused him to acknowledge the Huxleys while admonishing us to move further in and higher up in our understanding and use of the biological sciences in deciphering the human moral code. Wilson believes that the energies now held captive by religionists will one day be released for the service of scientific and ethical naturalism as the more convincingly correct mythos of the universe. When this happens, the human community will seek to do the right thing because it is the right thing to do for the universe, and not just because God said do it or because it serves the fundamental interests of the human species.

More than in any other place in Darwin's distinguished corpus of scientific writing, Wilson is here profoundly anticipated. Contrary to religionists' argument that without an external source of the moral code, humanity would be devoid of any sense of right and wrong, and, thus, would be reduced to savagery and violence. Often, when religious people enquire of the non-religious as to why they are good, these religious people are somewhat baffled to learn that non-religious people are good, that is, they do the right thing, because it is the right thing to do rather than out of fear of Divine retribution or punishment! The old 19th Evangelical slogan, "No morality without immortality," which suggests that people are only good in hopes of securing heaven, is, according to Darwin, the lowest form of human depravity. Darwin, Huxley, and Wilson had all rather claim that the moral code for humanity has been genetically generated through natural selection. In other words, the human moral code of conduct has evolved because it serves the best interest of the human community. Ethics and the moral code of human behavior have evolved directly in relationship to the need for speciel survival and, therefore, we do the right thing because it is the right thing to do. Ethical theism says we do right because God commanded it; ethical humanism says we do right because it serves the human agenda; but ethical naturalism says we do right because it serves the interest of the cosmos.

Wilson's entire career has been occupied with the task of integrating the sciences and humanities, particularly biological sciences and philosophy. His contention is that the separation of these trends in thought processes, in the search for knowledge, has been artificially created by the practitioners when the subject matter suggests integration, not separation. The term "consilience" is rarely used, until now thanks to Wilson, and dates from a time when the biological sciences and Darwin were just beginning to demonstrate the fundamental principle embodied in the term. While the Collier-Macmillan's *The Encyclopedia of Philosophy* fails to mention the term, Dagobert Runes' *Dictionary of Philosophy*, published by Littlefield, Adams in 1959, does mention the term and defines it as follows: "Consilience of inductions occurs when a hypothesis gives us the rule and reason not only of the class of facts contemplated in its construction, but also, unexpectedly, of some class of facts altogether different." While Wilson doesn't tell us how he found such a term, its redeployment in the service of integrating the various schools of human knowledge is a stroke of brilliance. His fascination with the concept is unbounded and his use of it to attack the arcane practice of discipline purity within the academy is outstanding.

Wilson's belief not just in the word but in its import is of two kinds -- first, this sort of integration of human knowledge through the convergence of the various disciplines of the sciences and humanities is directly proportionate to our increase in overall knowledge of the cosmos. The more we practice consilience, the greater our knowledge of the universe will be. And, second, the demonstration of the facility of consilience is the strongest possible argument for the "systematic integrality* (my term)" of the universe in which we live. Cosmic order rather than chaos awaits our discovery through the practice of consilience in the sciences and humanities.

The scientific agenda, of course, is the pursuit of empirically validated facts, correct information gleaned through the use of logic, reason, and experiment. The theological agenda, based upon "deep truths," or what C. S. Lewis calls in his *Chronicles of Narnia* "deep magic," falls outside the pail of scientific inquiry. The entire theological agenda, then, is based upon the notion of an outside agitator, an interventionist deity or divine source of caprice which periodically, erratically, and unpredictably operates in the world. Science, needless to say, can have no truck with such irrationality. If the cosmos is to be understood, it must be through the employment of the human mind, a mind governed by reason and logic, not deep magic. The theological agenda of the 18th century, and before and since, was predicated upon the duplicity of the universe, a dualism which allowed for logic and reason in all walks of life excepting in the world of religion,. In the religious worldview, faith took the place of reason, a faith-based dualism which allowed for the world to operate more or less along reasonable lines until religion substituted magic for reason to explain the will of the Church and that of the intervening deity.

The attempt on the part of the rationalists to keep some sort of transcendent reality while still embracing reason and logic led to a failed metaphysic called "deism." The deists wished to allow for a place in the universal scheme of things for a divine spark though not an intervening deity of the Christian variety. The failure of deism was its inability to mobilize the populous owing to its antiseptic, non-imaginative description of this divine source of all things. A God who doesn't reach down and fix things according to individual requests is hardly worth bothering with. Either God is personal, a Being with which I can have an intimate, personal, and passionate relationship, or God is worth less than a good insurance policy. Furthermore, deism couldn't promise the individual eternal life or salvation in the after awhile! And, finally, the basis of its ethics was sketchy and slight. Not relying on the evolutionary argument of the moral code being genetic and disavowing a personal Being of the nature of God in Christ Jesus, deism lost any attractiveness to those needing a personal relationship with the Creator God and One who would assure them of eternal salvation. Deism was simply too bland. It was a sort of science without evolution and a religion without God and neither option proved convincing, helpful, or nurturing.

The importance of the choice between a belief in the divine source of the moral code and the embracing of the genetic origins of moral behavior is monumental because it determines our understanding of who and what the human animal is and shall become. Either moral behavior is the results of a mandated code of conduct from outside the phenomenal world of biological evolution or it is a result of that biological evolution. If the moral code comes from out side, from an interventionist source derived external to the world, then the human animal is only responsible for following a set of laws handed down from above. However, if the moral code is genetically derived from the evolutionary process of natural selection, then the human animal is actually a participant in the process of its development. We are empowered to exercise jurisdiction over that moral code and to re-write it according to shifting situations in the world, always with an eye to do the right thing because it is the right thing to do for the environment. The first option, namely, an externally-derived moral code, disempowers and even exonerates the human community and the individual from responsibility or accountability beyond doing "what we are told." The second option, an internally-derived moral code, empowers the human community and the individual to decide ourselves what is the right thing to do based on our assessment of each situation. The subtlety and significance of this distinction cannot be over estimated. Either the moral code comes from outside or it doesn't. We can't have it both ways. Either the human animal is dependent upon the caprice of an interventionist deity or the human animal is responsible for devising its own code of ethics.

Wilson becomes profoundly prophetic in his portrayal of the great 21st debate, namely, whether we are to be transcendentalist or empiricist when it comes to determining the origins and nature of the human moral code, for this decision will determine the human agenda for the foreseeable future. Either moral behavior has biological roots or it has divine roots, and the distinction is monumental. The difference, however, between those who opt for transcendence versus those who opt for science is the

103

difference between an immaturity of needs/wants-based ethics derived from a father-god versus the maturity of the human willingness to accept and embrace our systemic integrality to the universe, wherein we act as a participating member rather than a temporary visitor to the world around us. This monumental distinction seems not only to be consistently true but indicative of a failed system of thought. The refusal or failure to identify the most fundamental "domain assumption" about the foundations of ethics -- whether from biology or from God -- both cheapens the ethicists' agenda and weakens their credibility in the consilient world of science and the humanities. Few would argue with what Wilson has suggested here in terms of the question of deism being fundamentally a "problem in astrophysics." That there is a biological God, a God known personally by individuals, who is intimately and directly, albeit sporadically and erratically, involved in the personal affairs of human beings in the world is most certainly destined to extinction within a very short time as the neurological and biological sciences close in on the last remaining arguments for such a God.

Wilson pits the present state of empirical studies of the relationship between moral behavior and brain function against the argument for a moral code based on transcendentalism using the argument that even though neurological science is still very busily working on the details of this biological reality in the laboratory, it is far removed from the personalistic and radical relativism of the transcendentalist school of religious thought. Here Wilson essentially dismisses the employment of a non-scientific concept called "Natural Law" as used by theologians and religious philosophers. The moral mandate for behavior is biological and genetic and has been codified because it worked, not because God established a "Natural Law" to which human beings must obey. The moral code is biologically generative rather than heaven-sent.

What is, however, exciting and hopeful is that present work within the framework of consilience between the behavioral sciences and biology will more fully development an understanding of the "primary origin" of moral behavior which evolves out of a dynamic interplay between "cooperation and defection." What in an earlier time was referred to as "moral sentiment" is now coming more fully into its own as a modern scientific concept again, based upon the realization that the interplay between biology and culture centers around the human animal (with possibly only the apes sharing this development) and our capacity to cultivate moral judgment and manipulate the interplay for the constructing of a complex matrix of codified moral behaviors.

Evolutionary biologists are now demonstrates profoundly the use of consilience in the integration of evolutionary biology and human culture. The interplay, the dynamic operative between the evolutionary emergence of moral behavior demonstrates the creative relationship between "moral aptitude" and the growing social awareness of the effectiveness of such behavior as a contributor to, indeed, a carrier of human survival, social and communal survival based upon and embodying the moral code implicit in such things as honor and justice and compassion. Rather than heaven-derived, these behaviors, which so centrally assure speciel survival of the human animal, are the product of the creative interplay between genetics and culture, between the biologically derived natural selection of survival behavior and culturally induced levels of cooperation and rejection, inclusiveness or defections.

Selectivity in moral sentiment is one way of accounting for the human animals' obvious preferences for its own kind, a commonly held worldview and ethos, and, unfortunately, the emergence of racism, prejudices based upon social, cultural, and physical differences within the species as well. The gradual emergence of warfare, national consciousness, political hierarchies, and religious dominations all are linked to this inborn propensity to moral behavior gone wrong. When the raw moral codes of behavior became susceptible to religious, political, and economic manipulation by those inclined to such domination in society, institutions of oversight and control -- religious, political, economic -- all emerged quite easily. Today, when philosophers, politicians, and religious leaders are in a position to dictate what can and cannot be explored in the science laboratory, there is little opportunity to unpack this fascinating matrix of ethics gone bad. The biological exploration of the moral sentiments, says Wilson, will one day give us a great insight into how we got this way and, hopefully, provide answers as to how we might move away from xenophobia and all that it has spawned in the religious, political, economic, and social matrices of human society.

To implement the methodology of consilience will provide a formal convergence of philosophical ethics and biological science to the study of religious behavior and ideologies, their emergence, their endurance, and their demise. When genetics and cultures are studied in their interplay through the use of biology and sociology, the human community will be the great benefactor. We will be better able to address problems and produce solutions which the interventionist ethicists are not able to provide using their notion of an externally revealed moral code. Natural Law seems not to have answers, only mandates as to what not to do.

Fear, control, and tribalism (read here xenophobic exclusivity) all serve the mission of the religious drive which is to stave off fear through the use of mythic narratives of tribal histories and protective gods. I have dealt at length with this phenomenon in my book, *"In the Beginning..."*: *Paleolithic Origins of Religious Consciousness*, where I have offered an extended psycho-cultural definition of religion complimented by Wilson's use of the term religion. As has been pointed out earlier in our discussion, religion is defined "as a complex of behaviors and ideologies consisting of rituals and myths which appeals to a transcendent legitimacy embodying a worldview and ethos addressing the verities of life and existence and conveying a dynamic level of psycho/social reality which is self-validating to the individual and community." This complex of behaviors and ideologies Wilson calls "tribalism."

Wilson's sociological and psychological insightfulness leaves many a sociologist and psychologist aghast by its profundity and simple genius. His critique of religion from both the sociological and psychological perspective easily stands alongside contemporary analysts such as Peter Berger and Clifford Geertz. Huxley strove valiantly but, alas, with little success to compete with the emotive strength and power of the religious myths with his creatively contrived arguments for ethical humanism. Wilson has chosen not to make that attempt but rather to continue steadily to promote the scientific worldview, its explanations based on empirical studies rather than philosophical and theological speculations about various and sundry hypotheses. The sometimes unavoidable sterility of the empirical sciences, competing against the emotionally charged and psychologically shackling power of the mythic tales, is matched by the sciences' use of reason and logic, methodology, and laboratory. Whereas religion has authority derived from the clergy who spin the tales promising eternal life, salvation, protection from the evil one, etc., science has authority derived from the empirical methodology of scientific inquiry. The former is emotional while the latter is rational, and, as Wilson points out, the human animal is an animal and susceptible to the passions and emotions of our own biological makeup.

The fundamental dilemma posed by transcendentalism (ethical theism) and empiricism (ethical naturalism) is not resolvable. It simply cannot be because the worldviews are based upon different and competing premises. The former draws from myth and passion, the latter from scientific inquiry. The evolution of the human mind, explains Wilson, favors belief in the gods because such beliefs serve the survival of the species by drawing groups together in the sharing of a worldview and the development of a mutually agreeable ethos. But of course, this evolutionary process dates from Paleolithic times. In the modern world where science has demonstrated the biological origins of religious belief, the continuation of a belief-system merely because it once served our needs but now deters maturation of human intellect is absurd.

The humble confidence of Wilson in the capacity of the biological and neurological sciences to explain the origins of moral behavior, indeed, to basically describe the biological nature of the human animal, is refreshing. Science, he says, can eventually teach us what we need to know the most, namely, why it is that human beings have evolved such that the embracing of one belief system rather than another, one moral code of behavior while abjuring another, happens. We need to know this and when we do we will be in a position to more fundamentally address the challenges facing the cosmos in the coming centuries. This we will know when the scientific and humanistic communities bring about a consilience in the study of gene-culture and evolution. The interplay between genetics and culture constitutes the arena for scientific enquiry.

Today's biologists are confident that scientific naturalism is gradually on the move in the mind of modern society and, they believe, the biological and historical epic of evolution, when told with passion, can be as captivating to the human imagination as any story in religious mythology. When awe, wonder, mystery and reverence are nurtured in the telling of the evolutionary epic of the cosmos, a deity will not be necessary to inculcate in the listener a deeply abiding sense of awe and wonder. Divine intervention or intrusion becomes a distraction and distortion rather than a reinforcement of the grandeur of the epic of cosmic evolution. The agenda should be to explore a multiplicity of ways to tell the evolutionary story, to make it come alive in the emotions and imaginations of the average person, to infuse its telling with the excitement known in the laboratories and the field studies of behavioral scientists. The story is tremendous but its telling must be equally so. The challenge of telling the story of biological evolution capable of soliciting such deep emotions is, really, a heuristic and pedagogical one rather than one of credibility. And, finally, the creatively told story must instill within the listener the grandeur of our place in the scheme of things. We are a partner and participant in the furtherance of the cosmos. It is a cosmic sharing which we must embrace, a vision of the connectedness of all reality, a systemic integrality of all things, not a god from outside the experienced world but a world reaching out for partnership with the human species.

Modern science's abiding concern, as we have seen throughout this analysis of Wilson's work and that of biologists everywhere, is towards the future, particularly how the human species finally defines itself on the basis of the two options of interpretation presently available to us, namely, religious transcendentalism or scientific empiricism. This choice, as we have pointed out over and over again, will determine not just the destiny of the human species but probably that of the cosmos itself since human beings are at least presently in a position to determine that destiny. Though the moral code of human behavior and religion itself are far more complicated than the current state of the natural and behavioral sciences are completely able to analyze, we do know that they are much more dependent upon the evolutionary process and the interplay between genetics and culture than either theologians or philosophers are ready to admit. As the sciences continue their unrelenting encroachment upon the historic domain of the religionists, religion itself will be increasingly forced to retrench, redefine, and reinvent the utility of its mythologies and magic in order to continue to stay viable as an operative worldview and ethos. As the human species becomes more and more scientifically educated and savvy, the perimeters of religion will continue to shrink. Inevitably, science will win and the secularization of the human intellect will necessitate the mobilization of that community in consort with the humanists to creatively construct a convincing mythology of evolution which will be both nurturing to the imagination and stimulating to an agenda of hope for the future of the cosmos. But in the meantime, religion will continue to market its wares of hope for eternal life, salvation, and the escape from planet earth to a heavenly abode with God and his angels. While that continues to hold sway within the human species, the science of evolution will continue its mission to untangle the mysteries of life.

The search for a new environmental ethic is, of course, what I have been suggesting all along, what I am calling "ethical naturalism." Wilson has not used this term but I am arguing that his science will produce such an ethic. Whatever we as a species finally decide to do with ourselves, our powers of creation and our powers of destruction, it is clear that we must make a choice about our future, whether ethical decisions will be attributed to a revelation from deity, or from our own best interests, or deciphered from the logic of the biosphere.

If we and the cosmos are to survive and prosper, we must turn our backs on ethical theism because it is pre-scientific and inevitably dysfunctional. We must turn our backs on ethical humanism because it places too high a value upon one species of life form in the cosmos. We must embrace an ethic which affirms the connectedness of all living things and our conjoined dependence up on the earth for our mutual survival. We must learn, through the development of a new environmental ethics built upon a genuine sense of the *systematic integrality** of the universe, that if the cosmos is to endure and we as participating members of that biosphere likewise, we must learn to do the right thing because it is the right thing to do for the cosmos, not for God, not just for Man, but for the Earth. We must identify, codify, and embrace an ethical naturalism designed the serve the best interest of the cosmos.

ETHICAL NATURALISM AND
COSMOLOGICAL EGALITARIANISM

Informed by Wilson's biodiversity and sociobiology, we have been suggesting that the primacy of the ecosystem is the fundamental infrastructure of ethical naturalism. It is the survival of the entire biodiversity of the cosmos which must constitute the proper focus of the human community, and not just some naïve fixation on "human survival" at the expense, if necessary, of everything else! By dismissing an archaic magical notion of an intervening God who, episodically, sporadically, and often irrationally, intrudes into the biological functioning of the cosmos, ethical naturalism is able to assert a rationalistic assessment of the proper functioning of ethical ideology and moral behavior. Furthermore, by building upon but going beyond ethical humanism, which determines ethics and morals based solely upon and within the context of humanity's well-being, ethical naturalism is empowered to assert the primacy of the ecosystem of the cosmos over merely humanity's welfare. Granted the high relevance of human worth, given our intellectual capacity to reason and act rationally, ethical naturalism espouses the primacy of the cosmic ecosystem even over the needs of the human person and the human community. Morality as the right thing to do exists because the Earth has said so -- the cosmos first and all else second is the mandate of ethical naturalism.

Systemic Integrality   Within the context of the "new morality" in E. O. Wilson's scientific naturalism, what has been called here "systemic integrality" simply means that the Universe itself is an organic confluence of logically linked functions which is essentially self-generative. Systemic integrality means that all functions within the Universe work systematically for the benefit of the whole -- thus, ethical naturalism simply means doing the right thing for the corporative benefit of the entire integrated system, namely, the Universe.

John H. Morgan

CONCLUDING POSTSCRIPT

Questions to ponder: Are humans genetically hard-wired to be religious? Are we hard-wired to be moral? Are these questions different? Does "religious" here mean specifically theo-centric? Might it just mean "eager for and susceptible to" a deep yearning for awe, wonder, mystery and reverence? Why are so many cultures and individuals devoid of a driving quest for a theistic worldview? Are non-theists deficient genetically or, are theists immature in their desire for an interventionist deity? Might theists and non-theists be genetically wired differently? Is it not possible that our genetic propensity to awe, wonder, mystery and reference is mistakenly thought of in monotheistic cultures as an instinctual desire for "God"? Might we all be simply instinctually drawn to awe, wonder, mystery and reverence but in theistic cultures we misinterpret this drive as God-centered rather than a human derivative?

Maybe "faith in God" as expressed in theistic cultures is really attraction/response to actual experience in the physical and social world of awe, wonder, mystery and reverence. Maybe it is institutionally-oriented religious practitioners who have captured, renamed and redirected our sense of the awe, wonder, mystery, and reverence propensities to service religiously devised institutional controls over the human community, collectively and individually. Maybe we are genetically wired to seek out and respond to awe, wonder, mystery and reverence and not to faith in a god at all. The question, then, is "Why are we awe, wonder, mystery and reverence-wired?" What purpose, evolutionarily speaking, do awe, wonder, mystery and reverence serve? Personally? Socially? Communally? Culturally? Politically? Paleolithic origins of religious consciousness do not imply a belief in God -- they do explain

113

the origins, however, of our susceptibility to awe, wonder, mystery and reverence.

To suggest that "faith in God" is "inherent to cultures worldwide and throughout history" (as suggested in an Oxford study being sponsored by the Templeton Foundation) is not synonymous with saying either (1) that religious faith in God is true, or (2) that faith in God is instinctual/genetic to the human animal. It only means (if proven) that human culture has evolved a propensity to institutionalize a human drive -- a drive which itself must be explored without theistic prejudices.

The danger in research on religion -- both behavioral composites and belief systems -- is the presumption that religious belief and behavior somehow always and automatically imply or require a deity. If precision is carefully exercised in the defining of terms, it is quite conceivable that religious belief and behavior could imply a pervasive sense of awe, wonder, mystery and reverence on the part of and within the framework of human experience of the world of physical and social environments without a deity at all.

Non-institutional expressions of awe, wonder, mystery and reverence may constitute a fertile ground for inquiry, namely, (religious) sensibilities and sensitivities devoid of a deity. The physical and social world may constitute the impetus for such emotions -- not a deity. Art, music, literature, poetry, community, athletics, politics, architecture, etc., may all provide mechanisms for expressing, fostering, and nurturing awe, wonder, mystery and reverence within the matrix of human experience. Is it possible that religiously devised institutions have misappropriated this human propensity to serve its own institutional interests?

As has been so boldly demonstrated by the work of E. O. Wilson, the biological and historical epic of evolution, when told with passion, can be as captivating to the human imagination as any story in religious mythology. When the deeply felt experiences of awe, wonder, mystery and reverence are nurtured in the telling of the evolutionary epic of the cosmos, a deity will not be necessary to inculcate in the listener such deeply felt experiences. Divine intervention may actually constitute a distraction and distortion rather than a reinforcement of the grandeur of the epic of cosmic evolution.

BIBLIOGRAPHY

Alon, I. *Socrates in Mediaeval Arabic Literature* (Leiden: Brill Magnes Press, 1991).

Attfield, Robin. *A Theory of Value and Obligation* (London: Croom Helm, 1987).

Badawi, Jamal. *The Foundation of Islamic Ethics* (NY: The Islamic Teaching series, 2008).

Barth, Karl. *The Epistle to the Romans* (NY: Oxford University Press, 1968).

Barth, Karl. *Anselm: Faith in Search of Understanding* (NY: World Publ., 1962).

Barth, Karl. *The Humanity of God.* (Richmond, VA: John Knox Press, 1972).

Barth, Karl. *Protestant Thought: From Rousseau to Ritschel* (London: Simon and Schuster, 1969).

Barth, Karl. *Church Dogmatics, Vols. I - IV* (Edinburgh: T. & T. Clarke, 1939-1960).

Barth, Karl. *The Faith of The Church* (NY: Mereidian Books, 1958).

Barth, Karl. *Evangelical Theology: An Introduction* (NY: Doubleday Anchor, 1964).

Barth, Karl. *The Humanity of God* (Richmond, VA: John Knox Press, 1972.)

John H. Morgan

Baier, K. *The Moral Point of View*. NY: Cornell University Press, 1958.

Broad, C. D. *Ethics and the History of Philosophy* (NY: Routledge & Kegan Paul, 1952).

Callicott, J. Baird. *In Defense of the Land Ethic: Essays in Environmental Philosophy* (Albany: SUNY Press, 1989).

Clark, Ronald W. *The Huxleys* (NY: McGraw-Hill, 1968).

Eastman, Roger. "Is Secular Humanism a Religion?," in *The Way of Religion* (NY: Harper & row, 1975).

Edel, A. *Method in Ethical Theory* (NY: Routledge & Kegal Paul, 1963).

Edwards, Paul (Editor in Chief), *The Encyclopedia of Philosophy*, Six Volumes (NY: Macmillan Publishing, 1967).

Fakhry, Majid. "Ethics in Islamic Philosophy" in his *Ethical Theories in Islam* (Leiden: Brill, 1994).

Fox, Warwick. *A Theory of General Ethics: Human Relationships, nature and the Built Environment* (Cambridge, MA: MIT Press, 2007.

Geertz, Clifford. "Religion as a Cultural System," in Michael Banton, *Anthropological Approaches to the Study of Religion* (London: Tavistock, 1968).

Hampshire, S. *Thought and Action* (London: Chatto & Windus, 1959).

Hare, R. M. *The Language of Morals* (Oxford: Clarendon Press, 1952).

Heschel, Abraham Joshua. *Man Is Not Alone: A Philosophy of Religion* (NY: Farrar, Straus, and Young, 1951).

Heschel, Abraham Joshua. *God In Search of Man: A Philosophy of Judaism* (NY: Farrar, Straus, and Cudahy, 1955).

Heschel, Abraham Joshua. *Man's Quest for God: Studies in Prayer and Symbolism* (NY: Scribner's, 1954).

Heschel, Abraham Joshua. *Who Is Man?* (Stanford, CA: Stanford University Press, 1968).

Heschel, Abraham Joshua. *The Prophets* (NY: Harper & Row, 1962).

Heschel, Abraham Joshua. *Between God and Man: An Interpretation of Judaism* (NY: Free Press, 1965).

Heschel, Abraham Joshua. *The Earth Is The Lord's and The Sabbath* (NY: Harper & Rowe, 1966).

Heschel, Abraham Joshua. *Who Is Man?* (Stanford, CA: Stanford University Press, 1968.)

Hourani, G. *Reason and Tradition in Islamic Ethics* (Cambridge: Cambridge University Press, 1985).

Hutcheon, Pat Duffy. "Julian Huxley: From materialism to Evolutionary Naturalism," *Humanist in Canada*, Autumn,

1999.

Huxley, Julian. *Evolutionary Humanism.* (Buffalo, NY: Prometheus Books, 1964).

Huxley, Julian. *Religion Without Revelation* (NY: Mentor Books, 1957).

Huxley, Julian. *Knowledge, Morality, and Destiny* (NY: Mentor Books, 1957).
Huxley, Julian. *Memories* (NY: Harper & row, 1970).

Huxley, Julian. *Evolution: The Modern Synthesis* (London: Allen & Unwin, 1942).

Huxley, Julian. *Evolutionary Ethics* (London: Oxford University Press, 1943).

Huxley, Julian. *The Uniqueness of Man* (London: Chatto & Windus, 1941).

Huxley, Julian. *Science, Religion, and Human Nature*, 1930.

Madigan, Timothy J. "Evolutionary Humanism Revisited: The Continuing Relevance of Julian Huxley," *American Humanist*, 2002.

Moore, G. E. *Principia Ethica* (London: Cambridge University Press, 1903).

Morgan, John H. *Being Human: Perspectives in Meaning and Interpretation (Essays in Religion, Culture, and Personality) Second Edition* (South Bend, IN: Quill Books, 2006).

119

Morgan, John H. "Ethical Humanism and the 'New Divinity': Exploring Post-Biblical Religion In a Secular World, or How to Spell 'Spiritual Relief'," delivered at the 2006 Oxford University International Studies Summer Programme in Theology.

Morgan, John H. *In the Absence of God: Religious Humanism as Spiritual Journey (with special reference to Julian Huxley)* (South Bend, IN: Cloverdale Books, 2006).

Morgan, John H. *"In the Beginning...": Paleolithic Origins of Religious Consciousness* (South Bend, IN: Cloverdale Books, 2007).

Morgan, John H. *Naturally Good: A Behavioral History of Moral Behavior* (IN: Cloverdale Books, 2005).

Morgan, John H. "Religion Without God: Exploring the Perimeters of Huxley's Humanism," in *Foundation Theology 2008: Faculty Essays for Ministry Professionals*, Edited by John H. Morgan (South Bend, IN: The Victoria Press, 2008).

Nowell-Smith, P. H. *Ethics* (NY: Penguin Books, 1954).

Piaget, Jean. *The Moral Judgment of the Child* (NY: Harcourt, Brace & World, Inc., 1932).

Prior, A. N. *Logic and the Basis of Ethics* (Oxford: Clarendon Press, 1949).

Rahner, Karl (Ed.) *Encyclopedia of Theology: The Concise Sacramentum Mundi* (NY: The Seabury Press, 1975).

John H. Morgan

Regan, Tom. *The Case for Animal Rights* (London: routledge & Kegan Paul, 1983).

Ross, W. D. *The Right and the Good* (oxford: Clarendon Press, 1930).

Shaw, Russell (Ed.) *Encyclopedia of Catholic Doctrine* (Huntington, IN: Our Sunday Visitor, 1997).

Singer, Peter. *Practical Ethics* (Cambridge: Cambridge University Press, 1993, 2nd edition).

Stanford Encyclopedia of Philosophy

Stevenson, C. L. *Ethics and Language* (CT: Yale University Press, 1944).

Taylor, Paul. *Respect for Nature* (Princeton: Princeton University Press, 1986).

Toulmin, S. E. *An Examination of the Place of Reason in Ethics* (London: Cambridge University Press, 1950).

Warnock, G. J. *Contemporary Moral Philosophy*. (London: Macmillan, 1967).

Wigoder, Geoffrey (Editor-in-Chief). *The Encyclopedia of Judaism* (NY: Macmillan Publishing Company, 1989.

Wilson, Edward O. *Biophilia: The Human Bond with Other Species* (Cambridge, MA: Harvard University Press, 1984).

Wilson, Edward O. *The Diversity of Life* (NY: W. W. Norton and Company, 1999).

Wilson, Edward O.   *The Future of Life*   (NY: Random House, 2002).

Wilson, Edward O.   *Naturalist: Edward O. Wilson* (Washington, DC: Island Press/Shearwater Books, 1994.

Wilson, Edward O. *On Human Nature.* Cambridge, MA: Harvard University Press, 1978.

Wilson, Edward O. *Concilience: The Unity of Knowledge* (NY: Vintage Books, 1998).

Wilson, Edward O. *The Creation: An Appeal to Save Life on Earth* (NY: W. W. Norton, 2006).

Wilson, Edward O.   *Sociobiology: The New Synthesis* (Cambridge, MA: Harvard University Press, 1975, 2000).

John H. Morgan

ABOUT THE AUTHOR
John H. Morgan, holds the Ph.D.(Hartford Seminary
Foundation), the D.Sc.(London College of Applied Science),
and the Psy.D. (Foundation House/Oxford), and is President
of the Graduate Theological Foundation and the Karl
Mannheim Professor of the History and Philosophy of the
Social Sciences. He has held postdoctoral appointments to
Harvard, Yale, and Princeton, and has been a National
Science Foundation Science Faculty Fellow at the University
of Notre Dame. He has been postdoctoral Visiting Fellow at
the University of Chicago and recently at the Center for Near
Eastern Studies at New York University. For a number of
years, he has taught a doctoral-level seminar at Oxford
University's international studies summer theology program
where he was appointed a member of the program's Board of
Studies in 1995 and began offering a course in the program in
1998. He holds a joint faculty appointment as the Sir Julian
Huxley Research Professor at Cloverdale College. The
author/editor of over thirty books in philosophy and the social
sciences, Dr. Morgan is a member of the American
Philosophical Association, the American Anthropological
Association, the American Psychological Association, and
the American Sociological Association and is a Senior Fellow
of Foundation House/Oxford. His latest book is titled
*Beginning with Freud: The Classical Schools of
Psychotherapy* (2009). In 2009, he was appointed to the
Advisory Board of the Kellogg College Centre for the Study
of Religion in Public Life at the University of Oxford and he
is also a member of the Advisory Board of the Oxford Centre
for Animal Ethics. Most recently, Dr. Morgan has been
invited to teach a course at Madingley Hall, Cambridge
University (UK). During 2010, he was a Visiting Fellow in
Islamic Studies at the Institute for Near Eastern Studies at
New York University.

Beyond Divine Intervention